BRAIDED STREAMS

Esther and a Woman's Way of Growing

by Marjory Zoet Bankson

LuraMedia

Artwork by Marjory Zoet Bankson.
(Monoprints created with ink on glass;
prints made on rice paper.)

International Standard Book Number 0-931055-05-9

Library of Congress Catalog Card Number 85-50203

Publisher's Catalog Number LM-602

Printed and Bound in the United States of America

LuraMedia™
10227 Autumnview Lane
P.O. Box 261668
San Diego, CA 92126-0998

*To Peter, my husband, and
Marcia Broucek, my editor,
who walked through this
with me.*

INVITATION **7**

1. HEADWATERS:
Four Different Streams Begin.... 13
    Esther's Story 14
    A Woman's Way of Growing....... 15
    The Streams of My Life 18
    Your Stream in the Story......... 20

2. CULTURAL CONTEXT:
External Images of Being Female... 23
    The King Speaks 24
    The Cultural Myth of Being Female ... 33
    My Reaction to Cultural Definitions ... 35
    Your Reaction to Cultural
      Definitions 36

3. NASCENT SELF:
Saying "No!" to Cultural Norms ... 39
    The Role of Choice: Establishing
      a Sense of Self 40
    The Role of Name and Story:
      Spiritual Identity............... 43
    Body Identity: Women and
      Violence 46
    Conflicting Images 49

4. SPIRITUAL HERITAGE:
A Larger Context for Life 55
    Connecting with Community....... 56
    Connecting Two Worlds........... 58
    Connecting with Dreams 62
    Opening to Mystery.............. 66

5. SEXUAL IDENTITY:
Internal Images of Being Female... 73
    Hegai's Influence 74
    Messages from Mother 77
    Messages from Father............ 82
    At Home in the Body 85
    Affirmations for Being Female 88

BIBLIOGRAPHY **173**

11. LIKE A RIVER FLOWING . . . 163
Esther's Story 164
A Woman's Way of Growing 166
My Life Like a River 168
Your Life Like a River 170

10. PARADOX OF POWER:
Esther and Public Violence 151
Choosing Violence 152
Community and Crisis 155
Celebration of Life 158

9. BREAKTHROUGH:
Esther as an Advocate 137
Extending Power 138
Staying Focused 142
Identifying Community 146

8. THE DINNER PARTY:
Facing the Enemy 119
Inviting the Enemy 120
The Role of Food 122
Haman's Discomfort 126
The King's Discomfort 128
God's Timing 131

7. STREAMS CONVERGING:
God's Presence as a
Body Experience 107
Fasting 108
Choosing Life 110
Esther's Reality 113

6. CHANGE OR DIE! 91
Different Views of Reality 92
Change as Threat 96
Time to Change 99
Making a Choice 101
Facing Mortality 103

INVITATION

As a stream emerges from a mountain onto flat land, it divides into several smaller streams that weave a braided path. Seen from the air, this braided stream spreads out from a single channel like a fan, winding its way through deposited sediment from the source toward the sea.

My childhood was like that mountain stream, emerging from the source body-centered and alive with joy. But, at puberty my sense of selfhood split into a braided path, into three different channels: sexual, vocational and spiritual. My sexual identity was shaped by what our culture said was female. My vocational ambitions were grounded in being a non-sexual "person." And my spiritual stream carried the mystical, imaginative and creative self that had no given form in the external world. My sense of self continued in that braided stream, winding its way through deposited sediment, from adolescence to midlife.

In nearly ten years of teaching classes in the School of Christian Living at Church of the Saviour, in Washington, D.C., I have learned that other women, too, have lived in braided streams between puberty and midlife. This book is an invitation to reflect on your own life experience as a braided stream.

When women measure their autonomy against the single ego stream that most men develop in the period between adolescence and midlife, women often feel scattered, wasted, meandering, depressed or frustrated. But as we begin to tell our own stories out loud and in books, in order to describe the patterns of experience among women, we can see that we are simply different from men. We can honor the diversity built into creation through our gender and recognize the creativity that is born out of those differences.

As I began to search the Bible for stories of women who embodied God among the people of Israel, I felt a sense of wonder at the many different ways that God entered human history. I also noticed that the differences between men and women who were committed to partnering often led to creative and humane action.

I came to the story of Esther through an assignment from the Women's Ministry of Faith at Work, an ecumenical renewal movement based in Columbia, Maryland. The Women's Ministry Steering Committee asked me to help design a weekend event around the issue of power for women. When the committee chose Esther's story as the basis for the weekend design, I was appalled!

As a Christian brought up in a Presbyterian Church in Bellingham, Washington, I was only slightly acquainted with the story of Esther. I knew she was the Jewish Queen who saved her people from a wicked plot by Haman. The only other thing I remembered about Esther was her beauty. Because she was stunning to look at, she was in a position to approach the king. Since I was neither beautiful nor did I approve of trading beauty for access to power, I did not turn to Esther as a Biblical account of God's revelation through the covenant people.

Esther's power was not a model for me, I thought, remembering the childhood version of her story. However, I got out my copy of the Bible, read all ten chapters of her story and found myself fascinated. It is a powerful and moving tale, rich with symbolism and drama, worthy of our time and attention.

The story of Queen Esther is a woman's tale of spiritual development. It contains many stages of self-discovery through which modern women can understand their own lives, both as a process of inward growth and outward action. Esther learned to say "Yes" to parts of herself in response to different men before she faced the crisis of death that brought her home to her own body as the way God could act to save her people. The story then describes how Esther expanded the sphere of her influence from her coherent center outward.

Heroic stories from the Bible have always been an important way for me to "get a sense" of what it means for a human to be connected with something larger, something beyond the self. Reflecting on Esther's story has been a way for me to connect my personal history with God's continuing presence in human history. The process of linking God's Biblical story with my own story became a conscious way of "doing theology" when I became involved with the Women's Ministry of Faith at Work. At a weekend Women's Event I attended in 1980, each participant was asked to write a spiritual autobiography. My own paper hinged on two questions: "Who am I?" and "Why am I here?" within the context of Biblical faith.

As we listened to each other share those papers, I realized how different our stories were from the conventional conversion stories with which I grew up. I began to hear that many women were conscious of a spiritual dimension in life at a very early age, but they separated that dimension from their sexual identity as females. I also heard tremendous conflict between sexual identity and ego identity "as a person," which sounded more like an effort to be accepted on equal terms with males. I began to wonder if women had a different pattern of spiritual development from men.

Braided Streams is a product of my wondering and observing. It is organized like a braid, weaving Esther's story with our collective story as American women, my own story and yours, which you are invited to add through the questions in each section.

Esther's story is part of the larger Biblical story, which Christians and Jews accept as God's revelation of purpose for all of creation. In a sense the Bible is God's answer to "Why am I here?". As we reflect on Esther's story and its connection with our own lives, we can expect to learn something of God and ourselves.

Our story as women is drawn from my own years of listening as a teacher and a counselor in both secular and religious settings. Since 1980, I have participated in many weekend Women's Events through Faith at Work which have given me intensive opportunities to hear women's stories. My hope for this book is that women will gather to share their own life stories around the questions posed in each section of the book, so we will not remain un-named and therefore un-blessed any longer.

I have included incidents from my own life at each juncture of Esther's story because that is finally how I test the truth of what I see and hear, just as you do. After all the words and pictures and ideas from others, I come home to my bodily experience to know what is true.

The questions about your life are meant to be private at first, requiring reflection and detail that may spill over into your day and night dreams. They are also meant to be shared with a prayer partner, spiritual guide or small group engaged in a spiritual journey together over time.

A word about translations I have used. The *Revised Standard Version (RSV)* of the Bible, which is commonly used by Protestants, is based on the Hebrew manuscript of Esther's story. *The Jerusalem Bible (JB)*, a French Catholic translation, is based on the fuller and more descriptive Greek manuscript. There is considerable debate about whether the Hebrew or the Greek manuscript came first and which is more authentic. Many scholars assume that the additional verses in the Greek version were added to make Esther's story more "godly." However, Bernard Anderson, well-known Old Testament scholar, suggests that details of court life in Susa, the city where the story of Esther took place, indicate that the Greek manuscript might have been written by a Persian Jew late in the Persian period of Jewish dispersion, around 300 B.C.* That would make the Greek version earlier than the Hebrew version.

Purim, the yearly Jewish festival commemorating Esther's story, was not known in Palestine until the Maccabean period, about mid-second century B.C., when Antiochus was trying to impose Hellenistic culture on Palestine. The Hebrew manuscript apparently dates from this period, when the story of miraculous deliverance was "good news" for the beseiged Jews.

Whether the Hebrew manuscript was the earlier written version or the Greek, Esther's story was so popular among Jews that there was no question about eliminating it from the canon scriptures. The Council of Jamnia (90 A.D.) confirmed Esther as a book in the Hebrew Bible, and it was accepted for the Christian Canon at Carthage in 397 A.D.

Because *Braided Streams* is not intended to be a scholarly exegesis of Esther, but rather an attempt to link God's story, our stories as women and my own personal story, I have chosen to use the fuller Greek version which can be found in *The Jerusalem Bible.* The basic story of Esther is found in any common translation.

The Interpreter's Bible, Vol. III, p. 827

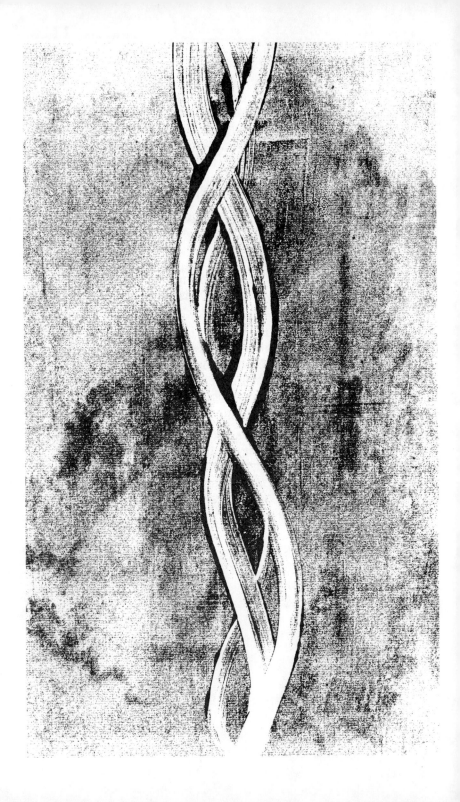

1. HEADWATERS

Four Different Streams Begin

There are four braided streams through the pages of this book: Esther's, ours as women, mine and yours. Each one has a different source. In the beginning each is coherent and body-centered, located in time and space.

Of the four interweaving streams, the most difficult to identify is the stream of our collective experience as women. Until recently, developmental literature used male experience to define the standard for ego development. In the past twenty years, however, women have begun to write of their own experience, and it seems to be different from what men have observed in women.

My thesis is that all women in our culture split their developing ego-consciousness into at least three streams—sexual, vocational and spiritual—during adolescence. Then, although we may identify with one stream more strongly than the others, we live out of all three until a major crisis or the natural development at midlife brings the three streams together.

Esther's Story

The story of Esther begins with an historical statement that locates it in time and space: "In the days of Ahasuerus." This indicates that the story was set during the reign of Xerxes, as the Greek manuscript called the king who ruled the Persian empire from 486 to 465 B.C. The Hebrew manuscript transliterated the Persian name as Ahasuerus. By either name, the Persian king ruled a mighty empire known for the famous legal code that governed both the Medes and the Persians.

After the fall of Babylon to Persia in 539 B.C., where the Jews had been in exile for half a century, the Persian king, Cyrus, had allowed groups of Hebrew exiles to return to Jerusalem and rebuild a modest temple there. Persian rule was benign, though expansionary, governing large territories through local military commanders and loyal political officials. By the time Xerxes ascended to the throne, artisans from various parts of the empire had erected a sumptuous capital at Susa on a tributary of the Tigris River. That is the setting for Esther's story.

The Interpreter's Bible notes the recent finding of a cuniform tablet from Xerxes' time with a name like Mordecai among the court advisors, so there is some evidence for the authenticity of the story. Many sources confirm the existence of a Jewish community in Susa, so it is quite possible that a crisis with the Persian rulers did occur.

Before that evidence was discovered, however, scholars took the story of Esther as a "festal narrative," told to justify Jewish celebration of a Babylonian festival. Some scholars, in fact, take Esther to be another version of the Sumerian myth of Ishtar, suggesting the name of Mordecai came from the Babylonian god, Marduk.* Whatever the source of the story, Jews have accepted Esther as an authentic portrayal of God's saving action from the mid-second century B.C.

The character of the Jews remaining in Susa influenced the story of Esther. Since the "faithful remnant" of the

---

*The Interpreter's Bible, Vol. III, p. 825.

Jewish nation would have gone back to Jerusalem, to the ruins of Solomon's temple, the ones who stayed in Susa would have been merchants and courtiers with learning or political skills, who continued their religious practices but did not identify themselves as the "nation of priests."

Esther's story has been told and retold as an example of the way God worked to deliver the Jews. The popularity of her story tells us something about the God of the Hebrews whom Christians also accept today. God did not choose the priests—the religious ones, the good and faithful ones—to embody God's presence and promise. Instead, God worked through the wily Mordecai and his beautiful cousin Esther— an unlikely pair for an unlikely purpose.

We can take the Biblical story as a literal record of how God acted through Mordecai and Esther, or we can understand the story as a metaphor of God's grace. Either way, it is a powerful woman's story through which to interpret our own lives. In Jungian terms Esther's story is a feminine counterpart to the masculine tale of Moses and the Exodus. Symbolically, Esther moved inward to meet God, while Moses fled to a far land. Esther entered the king's harem, left behind her mentor and religious community, then even her bodily safety, until she was stripped of all of her male protectors. She came face-to-face with God in her own "dark night of the soul." After that three-day period "in the tomb," she began to move outward from the centeredness in her own body, out into the world of public affairs.

A Woman's Way of Growing

Esther's story becomes our story as we recognize how her way of growing into self-awareness and ego identity is our way, too. Developmental psychologist Erik Erikson states that normal ego development moves from autonomy into relationships. Recently, Carol Gilligan has written about a different pattern for women. In *A Different Voice*, Gilligan states that a woman begins with relationship and discovers her autonomy through those relationships. We see that pattern of development in Esther's story, as well as in the feminine way in which she then proceeded to use her autonomy.

For reasons that are suggested in Esther's journey inward, a woman knows herself first through relationships with significant other men. Those relationships give way to autonomy at some point, often through some crisis, and a woman awakens to her singular identity and power. When that convergence comes, a woman brings richness and relational power into the river of her being as a autonomous person in the world. Then she is ready for relationship as an equal instead of a dependent.

During the seventies, women added a female perspective to every field connected with understanding what it means to be human. We have awakened to the image of God "created male and female" in Genesis, chapter one. Women have begun to write and speak, dance and draw the image of God in female form. In addressing the question of God's *full* image, we are discovering the fullness of our own womanhood as well.

If a woman's life is first defined through her significant relationships, then different people reflect back to her *parts* of her self.

One stream of being created as a woman is biological and reproductive. However, the sexual image of that body-centered female identity is shaped by our culture, and therefore by the language and interpretations of men. If creativity is right at the heart of being made in the image of God, then we must ask how to claim our creativity beyond bearing children. Our biological role is only part of the identity that we must integrate. Other streams must be explored as well. Now that women can expect to live nearly eighty years, we have *half* our lives to live beyond child-bearing years.

Another stream of our female identity is work in the world. Men have long claimed their creativity through work. Since bearing children is not an option for men, they have usually identified ego development with working for pay and being recognized by peers. "Women's work" has often been a euphemism for unpaid or menial work, as though bearing children was the only purpose for women in society. Limiting creative work opportunities for women has been a way to keep women from claiming their full creative potential. As women, we may hold the key to a more humane work world as we begin to affect the pay and recognition structures of our society.

Spiritual life is a third dimension of being a woman that our culture associates with intuition and emotion. It may be the stream in which we keep alive our sense of self-hood and body-reality when the other streams dry up or cause us to feel invisible. Whether the spiritual stream develops because other tangible forms of creativity are not available to us, or whether we are physiologically disposed to intuitive or non-physical input, it is clear that women are often open to spiritual matters at an earlier age than men. Churches are usually filled with women. That mystical or spiritual stream splits off from the scientific materialism of our culture, but it often serves to keep alive an image of self when the culture would confine us to children, church and cooking.

Between puberty and menopause, braided streams—sexual, vocational and spiritual—make it possible for women to compromise some of their own ambitions in order to protect children and support others emotionally. These separated streams that women seem to develop during adolescence (which male psychologists have often labeled as "immature moral development") probably make it possible for women to tolerate or even enjoy being with a two-year-old! But we are beginning to see that the frustration of living in those separated channels often brings explosive and sometimes angry energy to midlife.

At midlife American women are experiencing new life as the streams converge, unifying their separated channels into a powerful new force for change in our society. We are living at a time in history when women with enough energy, education and experience to affect our cultural patterns are entering public life with a vision of embodying the female part of God's image.

It is clear to anyone who looks at a daily newspaper that our public arena is suffering from a mechanical, hierarchical political structure that does not embrace diversity or change very well. Our world is suffering from the image of God as male only. Women are coming into public life at the very time when over-emphasis on masculine power and control could kill us all in a nuclear holocaust. Perhaps, as Mordecai wrote to Esther, we *"have been born for just such a time as this!"*

The Streams of My Life

My views about other women are, of course, influenced by my own experience. I grew up in a stable, loving family. My father was a family physician, born and raised in Lynden, Washington. My mother came from Arizona, met my father at Stanford, and worked in San Francisco before they married. She became a full-time mother when I was born, and two younger sisters completed our family unit.

At puberty my own sense of ego development was anchored in being a good student and a political leader in school and church. Always responsible, I was an eldest daughter in everything that I did.

As I entered the cultural milieu of junior high and high school and began to develop sexually, I wanted to be attractive and desirable as a female as well. My way of dealing with the dilemma of "besting the boys" at school was to date college students. In fact I kept my social life separated from my scholastic life until I met Peter Bankson during my senior year in college. We married a year later and, quite unconsciously, I put my sexuality in a box labeled "wife, reserved for owner." The "owner" was Peter, not myself.

My own spiritual development went underground during puberty. As a student of the pipe organ, I practiced in a mortuary and began to wonder about life and death. I began to ask questions about justice and God's power to help people in their daily lives. Asking those questions in silence made me think that God was calling me to the mission field. When I went to the minister of our local church, he assured me that my "call" would soon turn to thoughts of marriage instead of the mission field. I went away determined never to speak of my inward spiritual impulses again. My silence did not halt my searching; I kept my questions inside.

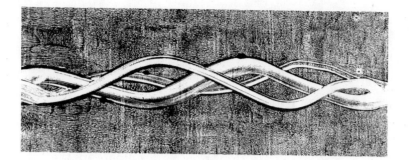

My life-line between puberty and menopause was a braided stream with three different channels. The mainstream during my teenage years began as a serious student, but I compromised my career ambition of becoming a lawyer in order to marry Peter. My vocational stream decreased in intensity during my twenties, when I was teaching high school history. In my thirties that stream intensified again as I became a professional potter, and now I see that my current work in retreat ministry combines both teaching and art into a highly creative and non-institutional vocational stream.

The secondary stream for me was a mystical creative strand that was encouraged by my mother through reading, music and home-making as a conscious creation. That stream was largely nonverbal and imaginative, expressed in music, knitting, clay and now writing. This creative stream carried my sense of self and body-awareness but, until recently, did not feel very grounded in my sexuality.

The third and least developed stream for me was my sexual identity, largely learned from watching my mother and grandmother as "neutered" older women and from the responses of adolescent males. I learned to see my sexuality from the standpoint of an observer and rejected the popular image of being a woman prescribed by our cultural values. Until recently, the sexual stream was my shallowest stream.

Now, these three streams have run together with increasing strength, but the story of how that happened will be part of our journey together in this book.

Journal Questions:
Your Stream in the Story

- Before you continue reading, take a few minutes to draw your life-line on a piece of paper or in your journal. Give it any form or direction you would like. Mark an $\times$ to show where you are right now and indicate major events, turning points or changes. At each of those points note your age and add + or a − for your feeling at the time.

- In another color add a second line to show your development of sexual awareness as a woman.

- Add a third line for the development of your mystical or spiritual life.

- Now look at the pattern created by your three lines. Notice where they intersect and where they separate. This is the braided stream of your life.

Save this drawing for reference. It will be useful as a starting point for other reflections on the braided stream of your life.

Conclusion

Esther began to live her braided stream by splitting her Jewish heritage from her life at court. In our own culture the headwaters of our stream as women began, especially during the past two decades, with questioning the standard patterns defined by males and then applied to the experience of females. The headwaters of my own "splitting off" into different streams began in junior high, when I kept my sexual development apart from the more important scholastic stream, and kept my wondering about God apart from the cultural norms in the church. The headwaters of your own life experience are important, too. Take a few minutes to reflect on your own experience during junior high and high school as the beginning of a braided stream in your life.

2. CULTURAL CONTEXT
External Images of Being Female

Every person is born into a cultural context of language and values. Our culture shapes our expectations for the future and our interpretation of history. We experience the impact of our culture through our parents and through the other influences that surround us: TV and radio, school, church and community. Before we have the language and thought patterns to understand and interpret these external influences, they shape our interpretation of reality. The cultural milieu is dominated by those who control the public form of language and laws. Cultural images of what it means to be female shape our self-understanding from the very first days of life.

For Esther, the king represented the cultural context of her life. Perhaps *his* version of the whole story of Esther may have been something like this:

The King Speaks

I'm in charge here!
Absolute ruler, some say.
It's true.

Three years into my reign
banqueting for six months
makes me bored. What's next?

Vashti smooth as a snake
ahhh...I love that stirring in me

Why not...why not show her to my commanders now?
She's ripe and luscious.
They can't touch...
she's mine...
silky smooth skin mouth hair...

Go get her for me!

* * * *

What?
She won't come?
Why not?
She said no?
What the...

Shut him up will you, Memucum?
The king's making a fool of himself
Quiet down
and let's think.

Everyone'll know
*   that she refused to come*
*   because the women know*
*   and we can't keep them all*
*   quiet.*

Kill her? Maybe that's not
*   the wisest thing. Think.*

Keep him quiet will you, Meres
Why did he drink so much?
*   Why did you let him?*
Let's think.

The law says
*   she must perform*
*   any command of the King.*

She's wronged all of us,
*   not just the king.*
All women
*   will rebel and look down on us*
*   if she's kept around.*

Put her out.

Let the dogs have her.
*   Make it an order of the king.*

I like that.
Then they'll know who's boss.
Nobody can make a fool out of me.
She should have come.
I wanted her.

Why didn't she come?

Anyway, they'll find somebody else.
There are plenty of beautiful virgins
for me to have my pick.

I'll find one
just as good as Vashti
   smooth sleek skin
      better even than she was.

Why didn't she come?

So the search for a new queen began. Like a spoiled child the king waited for his advisors to find someone better than Vashti, someone who would come when he called.

When Esther's turn came, the king liked her better than Vashti, whose body he had almost forgotten in the year or more since that scene in the banquet hall. In fact he loved Esther so much that he crowned her queen and gave another great banquet in her honor. He lowered taxes briefly and gave gifts liberally to celebrate finding her among the many virgins who shared his bed for one night.

Intrigue continued to swirl around the king, who was governed by his passions more than his wit. Queen Esther proved to be a guardian of his safety when she told him of a plot by two of his eunuchs to kill him. The king was just glad to be alive.

When questioned for the record, Esther named Mordecai as the source of information that saved the king's life and it was recorded in the Book of Chronicles. The king did not question her connection with the Jew. He did not ask such questions. The king let his advisors tend to particular matters of state, like recording loyal deeds for future reference.

One of the king's advisors, Haman the Agagite, seemed to be a capable man, so the king promoted him above all the other advisors. Haman was given the right to decide how he wanted other people to treat him. Haman wanted everyone to bow upon seeing him, to remind them that he was in charge. Everyone in Susa bowed except Mordecai.

Haman was furious! What right did that Jew have to refuse an order? Mordecai's refusal triggered Haman's revenge. The Jews were different from other conquered people in the Persian empire. They had their own laws. They didn't worship the Persian gods. They didn't worship the king. Haman knew that fact alone would anger the king enough to agree that the Jews should simply be eliminated.

The king was not a vicious man. He was interested in stability and order in the empire. When Haman told him that there was a group of people scattered throughout the kingdom who refused to honor the laws of the kingdom, the king was concerned. Such resistance could lead to rebellion! The king agreed that Haman could eliminate these people. He did not care very much. They were of no great consequence to him. In fact, he didn't know any Jews and could not remember meeting any during his campaigns. So he signed and sealed Haman's order and returned to his life of pleasure without another thought.

The king enjoyed his unending supply of beautiful young virgins, and he did not share his bed with Queen Esther very often. Still he felt safe in the knowledge that she guided the affairs of his concubines and was a good hostess when he was entertaining on state occasions. She obviously had good connections outside the palace, for she was aware of political affairs, but she did not gossip or give advice unless he asked for it.

In fact, Esther was a good wife. She helped him and she did not ask for any special favors. She came when he wanted her. The king was generous with Esther and she seemed happy enough. And why not? She had everything a woman could want.

The king gave Esther whatever she wanted because she kept herself to the women's realm, until the day when she appeared unbidden in the Court.

What a shock!
No one was allowed to intrude without an invitation,
not even the queen!

At first I was furious!

HOW DARE YOU COME HERE!

Why had she come?

WHAT DO YOU WANT?
YOU HAVE NO RIGHT...

Why did she come?

Then she began to faint.

ESTHER! COME!

I held out my scepter
and her maids supported her
and she came.

Why did she come?

"Will you and Haman be my guests for dinner?"

Why did she come?

"We will come."

Haman and I had a wonderful time, drinking wine, telling stories and admiring Esther's beauty, but she didn't say what she really wanted. She asked us back for the next night, just the two of us, and we were delighted.

Esther served the meal herself and I thought, "We must do this more often. It's not the same old war stories, talking with Esther like this. She is so...ummm...what would the word be? Haman and I are lucky that she wants to entertain us again tomorrow night."

Why am I so restless tonight?
  Here, bring me a light and something to read.
    Ah yes, the Chronicles.
      That will put me to sleep...

What's this? Oh yes, Bigthana and Teresh... good thing we had them hung. No good eunuchs...trying to kill me. Have to keep your eyes open all the time. Who put us wise to their plot? Someone named Mordecai. Don't remember that name. Not on the staff. Wasn't there some connection with Esther? Maybe that would be a way to honor her.

Wonder what she wants?

She never asks for anything.

I like her.

She's always been nice to me.

I'll do that. I'll ask Haman in the morning for some way to honor that man who told Esther... where's his name again... Mordecai?

I talked to Haman the next morning. He had a good suggestion about parading the honored one around on a horse wearing the king's robes on his shoulders. I ordered Haman to honor the man named Mordecai just that way, and then I went to get ready for Esther's banquet. "I'll send

Haman home early," I thought, "so we can have some time together. I'll tell her about honoring Mordecai then and see if she likes that. She is intriguing. I wonder what she wants..."

That evening we came to Esther's chambers for another banquet. After we had eaten and were drinking wine together, I felt mellow and full of Esther's fragrance. I asked once again what she wanted. I could not imagine what it might be. She really had everything.

She stood silently for a moment, as though listening to something inside of her. Then she spoke:

"I ask for my life, and that of my people," she said.

Everything stopped.

"What?"

"We have been sold, I and my people. We are to be slaughtered, soon. If only we had been sold into slavery, I would have kept quiet. But we are to be killed. I ask for my life, and for that of my people."

"How can that be? Who ordered that?"

"Haman!"

I was stunned!
I could not think.
Quick, get outside.
Collect yourself.
Think man!

Wish I hadn't drunk so much.
Haman, chief of my advisors.
How can that be?

Wait, I remember now,

Haman said there were some people
    who didn't obey my laws.

I signed the eliminating orders and sealed them myself!

I want to help Esther.
She's always come when I desired her.
She saved me from that palace plot.
She's been kind to me, given me whatever I wanted.

How can I undo that edict?

There's no way.
Now that it's sealed, it's done.
Think man.
Think!

When I came back into the room, I couldn't believe my eyes!
There was Haman, sprawled on the Queen's bed!
Was he going to rape her before my very eyes!
Has he no shame?
No limits?

I must have been shouting, because the guards came
running and dragged Haman away. One of the eunuchs
said that Haman had erected gallows on which to hang
Mordecai, so I directed them to use it for Haman instead. At
least that was one problem out of the way!

What a day!
Haman hanged on his own gallows.
Esther told me Mordecai was her own adopted father.
I gave Mordecai the signet ring that Haman used
and I gave Esther the right to set Mordecai in Haman's place.

The rivalry between Haman and Mordecai goes back to a feud between the Hebrews and the Agagites in the time of Moses in Egypt, I found out, so I am not going to worry that it was something I should have known about. It's the kind of thing one can't control. Mordecai saved me once. He raised Esther. I trust him, at least for now.

What's this?
Esther again?

"What is it, my dear?"

"Your people? Still in danger?...
Oh yes, I remember. Haman's edict can't be changed.
Have Mordecai think of something.
No, of course I don't want them to be wiped out.
Have Mordecai think of something.
I'll sign it."

So Mordecai sent an edict to all the provinces of the kingdom, setting a day when Jews could arm and slaughter their opponents. That seemed fair enough. It cost me nothing. They did not seem interested in taking riches, only lives of their opponents, so I am satisfied that it was for the best.

Esther asked for another day of killing in Susa, to hang Haman's ten sons and let everybody in the capital know that Haman's power was finished. Then the Jews set a time to celebrate and give thanks for their deliverance. It seemed

*like a nice way to honor Esther, so I gave Mordecai
permission for that, too.*

It's still hard to give Esther anything.
She never asks for herself.
She always defers to Mordecai.
I wonder if it's their religion.

No matter.
It doesn't seem to hurt anything.
She always comes when I want her.
She doesn't look down on me.
I remember the advisors warned me against
letting a woman have any power at all.
They said women would look down on men
    if men gave women a choice.
Esther still respects me.
The advisors were wrong.
At least they were wrong about a woman
    like Esther.

She comes when I want her.
That's enough.

The Cultural Myth of Being Female

The king personifies the cultural myth of man over woman
as the "natural order" of creation. The king was driven by his
desires and entrapped by laws of his own making. Acting as
though he had no personal connection with the forces at
work in his kingdom, the king sounded like some of our own
leaders. He sat at the top of a pyramidal power structure,
interested only in his control.

Like some rude caricature of true leadership, the king was trapped by the system he had helped to create: laws could not be changed; advisors protected the king instead of the people of the kingdom; and power simply meant control over other people's lives. It was a static, closed system with a high premium on obedience.

The king reflected back to Esther a picture of being female that was clear and rather simple. He wanted her body and her talents when it suited him, for his own pleasure. It did not occur to him that she was a person with any right to choice or change.

The king was ruled by his passions, but his feelings were disconnected from his thinking process. Throughout the entire drama the king remained unconscious of others. He was something of a cardboard character representing ownership and control. His reaction to Haman—"What! Is he going to rape the Queen before my very eyes?"—was the cry of a child whose toy was being taken away.

We do not need to look far to see the "king" in our own culture. His image of what a woman *should* be speaks from every seductive billboard, TV advertisement, newspaper comic strip, magazine rack and porn shop. Think of the images we see every day, telling us what it means to be a woman.

Those images provide the background for an operative cultural value system that keeps women from developing their full creative potential. Those words and pictures shape our thinking about necessities, possibilities, and survival needs; and place limits on actualizing the spiritual and vocational yearnings that we all have.

The king's interpretation of Esther's story is the cultural environment we live in, too. The king's emphasis on outward control has been abstracted into technology, and the same drive to control others permeates our public values. The king in our own culture controls records, official language and physical life, too, which makes it difficult to interpret events from another standpoint. As long as our culture functions with a hierarchical and mechanical system for valuing life, women will be treated like some inferior lifeform.

My Reaction to Cultural Definitions

When I think of the many images of being female that I see every day, I feel angry or detached. Most of those images do not describe me. I am neither a dumb and dreary housewife worried about the ring around my bathtub, nor am I a sexy Revlon siren. Some of the public images of being a woman are positive, but most have a shallow quality, as though there were no real person there, only an object—something to be used or looked at or cuddled with.

The female members of my family gave me a different picture about being female. They expanded the number and variety of cultural images for me. My mother read a lot and nurtured my imagination through books and writing, but I rejected her pattern for being female because she chose illness instead of claiming space for her sexual or vocational ambitions. My grandmother was strong and care-taking in her version of being a traditional mother, but she stayed within the tight boundaries of her Dutch immigrant background. Neither woman gave me any clues about dealing with my sexuality.

As a result, the "Don'ts" of parental fear—that I might get pregnant or get involved with the wrong kind of male friends—became my guide for being female in our culture. When I "got my period" (like some dreaded disease), I felt my body had become an adversary who might get me into trouble. In reaction to the shallow pictures of being female in our society, I stayed emotionally detached from my sexuality, although I trusted my body feelings as a deep source of truth.

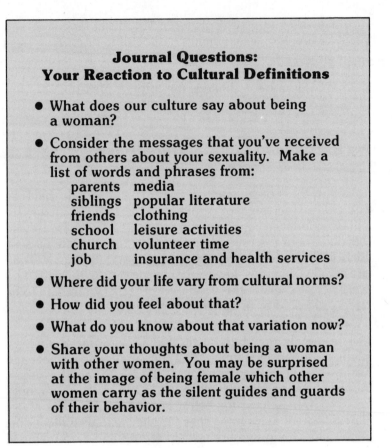

Journal Questions:
Your Reaction to Cultural Definitions

● What does our culture say about being a woman?

● Consider the messages that you've received from others about your sexuality. Make a list of words and phrases from:

parents	media
siblings	popular literature
friends	clothing
school	leisure activities
church	volunteer time
job	insurance and health services

● Where did your life vary from cultural norms?

● How did you feel about that?

● What do you know about that variation now?

● Share your thoughts about being a woman with other women. You may be surprised at the image of being female which other women carry as the silent guides and guards of their behavior.

Conclusion

The cultural context which the king represented taught Esther to affirm only part of her life: that which others valued. The king symbolized the Persian culture in which both Mordecai and Esther lived. The king in our culture permeates our lives through language and laws, customs and institutional structures. As Americans, we live in a culture that proclaims equality for all and, yet, expects subordinate behavior from women. The difference between spoken ideals and customary behavior gives women conflicting images about being female, but the professed ideals do contain the possibility of change and partnership.

3. NASCENT SELF

Saying "NO!" to Cultural Norms

Alone she stood, eyes flashing, manicured hands still at her sides, while seven eunuchs from the king stared at her in disbelief: "No!" Vashti repeated through clenched teeth, "I will not come!"

At the gateway to Esther's story stood the woman who was queen before her. Vashti was banished before Esther was chosen to be queen. According to *The Jerusalem Bible,* Vashti was "unknown to history," except as a Biblical prelude. She left a space for Esther, but her story lives as a part of the setting for Esther's accession to power. Vashti was Esther's foremother and ours as well. Her nascent, or beginning self, was born prematurely in a moment of crisis.

The Role of Choice:
Establishing a Sense of Self

Vashti's part of Esther's story opens with an elaborate description of the sumptuous Persian court and a six-month-long celebration of King Xerxes' many victories. The scene of Vashti's refusal is set at the end of a week-long banquet.

The banquet scene began with a description of choice about drinking which the king extended to all the male visitors. The king provided ample wine in golden chalices for all the celebrating warriors, but no one was forced to drink. The king gave men a choice about whether to receive his gift or to refuse it. Autonomy was granted to them, but Vashti had no such choice. "On the seventh day, when the heart of the king was merry with wine, he commanded...the seven eunuchs...to bring queen Vashti before the king with her royal crown, for she was fair to behold" (Es. 1:11, *RSV*).

When the eunuchs came to get her, Vashti refused to come!

When the king heard of her refusal, he was enraged! The king's council gathered to advise Xerxes after his anger had cooled. They warned him that Vashti's disobedience would set up instability all over his kingdom. "The wives of all the Persian and Median administrators will hear of the queen's answer before the day is out...that will mean contempt and anger all around" (Es. 1:18, *JB*). The men clearly believed that Vashti's choice was a threat to them.

So Vashti was banished and the news was carried throughout the kingdom! What happened to Vashti was meant to be a lesson other women would not forget. They knew that Vashti had rejected the unspoken trade of sexuality for physical security. Vashti's elimination was meant to warn other women against doing what she had done. But, her action implied that there was something more important in her life than existence alone.

Vashti rejected the cultural image of what a woman should be and how a woman should behave. She had been entertaining the wives of visiting dignitaries, and her guests must have heard her refuse the order to appear, for later the king's advisors considered the rebellion that might result when the commander's wives returned home. But no crowd could protect Vashti from the king's anger; she was banished and her name was stricken from court records.

Men assumed that they had the right to choose, but that women did not. Vashti challenged the male interpretation of right by making a choice for herself. She asserted a different view of nature! "I do not choose your system or your control," her actions said. Her choice confronted the myth that a man had the right to order and control a woman at home or in public.

Vashti was not made queen because of her assertion of her right to choose. From the very beginning she was a beautiful, capable and very *cooperative* role-model for women in that kingdom. While the king was entertaining his princes and servants in the palace gardens, Vashti was doing the same for the women. She was being a good "corporate" wife!

Something tipped the balance for Vashti. Something in her shifted, and she said "No" to the cultural demands on her life. Her refusal was an act of ego definition. The result was punishment: she lost her position in the male world. She gave up her vocational identity in order to establish her sense of self.

How different is our culture today? We also expect free choice from males, even young ones, but do not expect or want the same from women. Instead, women are taught to obey and adapt at home and at work in order to preserve relationships for their own protection.

Parents train us to be docile and attentive to the tone of voice, cooperative in the name of safety for our prettiness. Vashti knew that, too. She was the king's, to have and to hold, a gem to show, an object for others to admire and envy him for having. What angered the men was her freedom of choice: she was acting like a person, not a slave.

Vashti stood alone, protecting something more valuable to her than pleasing the drunken king and his court. What was it? We pick up the newspaper and read the stories of rape and abuse. We hear the sounds of laughter and bragging, locker room jokes from jaded men. We recognize the hatred spilling from pornographic magazines, and we know the truth about alcohol and domestic violence. We know what Vashti was protecting with her strident "No!"

Vashti is part of Esther's story and my story and yours, too, as she stands alone, surrounded by a circle of seven unbelieving men who were shocked that she refused to cooperate with their view of right. "Come," they urged, "the king wants you to come so that all the men at Court can see how beautiful you are."

As I read Vashti's story, my stomach churns and my breath tightens. I see myself standing alone on a street-curb in Bangkok, Thailand, in 1967, waiting for the bus. The one who would have protected me simply by being an American man, is lying in a hospital bed at the other end of the alley. As I stand there, two drunk American soldiers are trying to make me come with them, touching, talking, making suggestive sounds, pushing, one on each side. I freeze, rigid and silent, staring at the road, waiting for the bus.

I feel movement around me and panic clutches at my throat. Other bodies press around me front and back, checking any movement. Then I see what is happening: without a sound, the chest-high Thai men and women are lending their strength to my refusal.

We wait together, while the GI's continue to pull and to talk with their beery breath, irritated by the other bodies standing close around me. Finally the bus comes and I breathe deeply as my foot feels the step. I move quickly up and away from torment into safety as brown faces smile, making room for my whiteness as the bus pulls away from the men on the curb.

Vashti's story, meant to be a warning against saying such a "No!," has just the opposite effect from what was intended. It gives me an invitation to say "No!" when my body is about to be violated. I feel proud of Vashti's refusal. I love her reckless strength. I know the cost of such replies, where brute strength and economic power threaten life itself sometimes, but something in her act meets longing in myself.

Vashti's "No!" helps me define the edges of my own ability to choose for my body-self in a hostile environment.

Our cultural myth suggests that if we cooperate and play the female role according to the rules, then nothing bad can happen. There is an implied contract that if we will just believe hard enough and just behave "good enough," then no harm will come. We ignore the fact that Jesus' belief did not protect him or the disciples from violent death. The cultural myth is not enough to bring us safety.

One way we can begin to name the ways in which women are confined and degraded is by speaking out of our own experience. Our silence works against us, protecting the structures that encourage violence between sexes.

Journal Questions:
The Role of Choice

- Picture yourself in Vashti's place, standing alone with men of authority in a circle around you, demanding that you come with them . . .

- How would you react?

- What might you say or do?

- Describe any feelings or images that Vashti's situation arouses in you.

The Role of Name and Story:
Spiritual Identity

Vashti became "unknown to history." Erased. Disappeared. Men controlled history by controlling the records of public life. Presumably Vashti was "known to history" while she was queen. The power to rewrite chronicles, or historical records, belonged to the men of the court. The power of language could thus be kept over time and distributed over space for the purpose of influence and control. Vashti's name could be eliminated from history to suit the needs of those in charge. Does that mean her life had no meaning?

Women have struggled to value their lives without the benefit of access to public records and legal rights. In *The Underside of History,* Elise Boulding has reconstructed a history of women and their contributions to human culture, using fragments like this story of Vashti, because official records have usually ignored the role of women. Was it because men did not think that women were fully human? Or if human, then not quite as developed as persons? Is that a spiritual issue?

Every woman starts life in our culture with her father's name, perpetuating a sense of being his property until she is turned over to another man. This "belonging" works subtly against our independent sense of self. Until the time is right to choose life against the threat of spiritual (or physical) death, we keep our spiritual stream inside like a secret spring. We operate in the world through the name of father and husband, while our personal names become a way of keeping us "one of the girls." The role of finding one's "true" name and establishing one's own personal story, therefore, becomes the core of a woman's spiritual quest.

Being named and having a name speaks of cultural heritage and belonging in a family. It is an important aspect of personhood. Today we read about Argentine women who stand each week in silent vigil with pictures of their children who have "been disappeared" by the police. They are bearing witness to the reality of those children by showing the names and pictures in public. Those women are refusing to let official records be the only source of truth in Argentina. Amnesty International performs a similar task, keeping track of political prisoners by name to keep alive the spirit of ones who have "been disappeared" by secret police.

Many of us have read George Orwell's novel, *1984*. In it he deals with the theme of name and public records. He dramatically outlines how public record, written and re-written, affects our interpretation of events by affecting the context in which things happened. "What *really* happened?" we ask. "What is my *real* name? Who are my parents?" And by implication, "Who am I?"

When we are young, the power to name belongs to adults. It is a powerful means of control that many of us use unthinkingly. Because my dad was overseas in World War II when I was a child, I never learned to take teasing from him. When he came home safely, we went through a painful period of reacquaintance. When dad would call me "George" or "Sam," I remember panic would flood my throat until I fled the table in tears. "What's the matter with her?" he'd ask.

My name was gone! It wasn't just some friendly hide-and-seek game he was playing, but a joke I could not understand or defend against. I was not *me* anymore if he did not name me with the right name. I ran away because I could not defend myself against his casual obliteration. I learned to say "No!" to his power over me by leaving the scene. What happens to those little girls who cannot run away?

I believe that grave damage is done to the spirit of any child who cannot protect the sanctity of nascent self being born through saying "No." In running from the table, I learned to say "Yes!" to my own spiritual identity. It was the first step in learning to name myself.

Many years later, when I was beginning to make pots and literally scratch my name into clay to mark each one as my creation, I wanted to use my maiden name, "Zoet," because it was short and distinctive. But I was afraid that it would hurt my husband's feelings, so I never talked with him about the choice. I simply used my married name, "Bankson." By doing that I gave away my power to choose my name and therefore to claim some part of my full identity.

I realize now that making pottery was part of my spiritual stream, flowing out of the inborn desire to be creative, as God is creative through us. When I began potting professionally at the age of 31, I said "Yes" to my spiritually-creative stream inside and gave my "Yes" physical form through pottery. Not to ask the question about my name in clay meant that I had not yet taken the power of choice that Vashti exerted in her refusal. I had not yet brought my spiritual-creative stream together with my own vocational and sexual streams. I had not yet learned to name myself from the inside out.

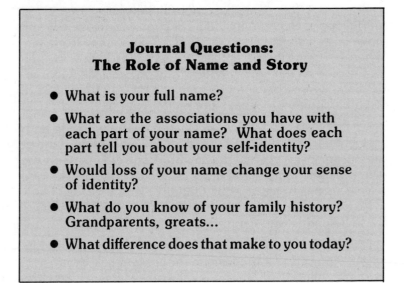

Journal Questions:
The Role of Name and Story

● What is your full name?

● What are the associations you have with each part of your name? What does each part tell you about your self-identity?

● Would loss of your name change your sense of identity?

● What do you know of your family history? Grandparents, greats...

● What difference does that make to you today?

Body Identity: Women and Violence

Vashti's story began with a celebration of military conquests and ended with her banishment. Vashti was not simply a victim of male dominance; she did assert her right to choose for her own sense of self. She did not change the way that women were treated within the political system. She could not protect herself, and she did not see her actions within a larger spiritual context. She was judged and condemned for disobedience, and banishment made her an outcast without protections of any sort.

If Vashti had not lived in a violent society, being dismissed would not have threatened her life. Being without a husband in that society, however, made her fair game for any man. Violence and power were controlled through the legal system. Women got along by adapting to that view of life. They were kept and protected like another lifeform, meant to pleasure and entertain men. Women traded their sexuality for security, and the laws were enforced to maintain a rigid balance of public security and private insecurity.

Like Vashti, we also live in a violent society in which men do brutalize women. We must not fool ourselves into thinking that independence will be rewarded by men who have depended on dutiful women, or that self-actualizing decisions have no fatal consequences. Women learn as little girls that such independence will not be tolerated. Laughed at or punished for independent behavior, girls usually respond by curbing nascent autonomy and giving up the aggressively independent ways that are encouraged in little boys.

Childhood mobility is often limited for girls, because a parent fears the child will be sexually molested or that the parent will lose control. It hardly matters what the motive is, for the effect on a girl is the same: she waits for permission to do what boys are expected to accomplish.

Learning the "rules" about being female came hard for me. I was the oldest of three girls and there were no boys in the family. I was tall, strong, responsible and independent. I felt at home in my body, enjoyed sports and was beginning to learn how to take teasing when I got to the fifth grade.

The year I was eleven, I grew to my present height and "got my period"...got an adult library card...stood with my bike and watched Little Leaguers play without me because I was a girl. And that year I knocked a boy down and gave him a bloody nose in my first and only fist-fight! Our fight escalated into a furious snowball fight between the boys and the girls.

Mr. Thompson, my fifth grade teacher, reacted drastically! The whole class was forced to spend playtime inside for a week. I felt responsible for what happened because we were all punished for the passionate eruption of that day. I learned that boys could fight, but girls must not. After that incident I thought my only choice was to stand silently like a stone when teased and never fight back. I did not learn to fight with words either, because that was not allowed at home.

As I grew older, I learned to avoid confrontation directly. I learned to say "Yes" to my own self with the risk of punishment, but not banishment. My own memory goes back to that modern ritual of adulthood, getting a driver's license.

"You're not ready to drive," I can still hear my father saying the night before my sixteenth birthday. I feel my shock and grope for words. "You need to take a driver's ed course first."

Stunned, I feel the tears form and fight them back. "But you never said that before. I thought I was doing it right. You've said so yourself. Why didn't you tell me that last fall?"

He didn't say a word, as though I hadn't spoken. We all sat silently at the dinner table, picking at our food. Mother coughed and cleared away now-empty serving bowls. I could not look at him, for fear I'd cry. The stoic in me braced and barely breathed until he left the table.

Later, in the kitchen my tears burned silently until my mother saw. She patted me lamely on the shoulder: no one crossed my father when he made such a pronouncement.

Then a wild thought came. Before I could catch it, words formed in the air: "Would you take me down tomorrow to see if I could pass the driver's test? If I can't, I'll wait and take driver's ed next spring."

She looked at me, surprised. We both waited for her answer.

"I'll pick you up after school," she said quietly.

Vashti stood there, impulsive and strong with us just then. We both knew it was wrong to go against my father's word. But without discussing it, we agreed to do it anyway.

When I passed the driver's test and came home with my

license the next day, my father simply accepted it with no further comment. My apprehension told me that I feared the worst, although I could not have told you what that was. Even now, my body tightens in response to that story, and I know that my body still records the message that it was wrong to be so secretive about opposing him. I did not know any other way to choose for myself, against my father. Wanting to obey and disobey at the same time was the bind that separated the different streams of my self.

What are the messages you received about protecting your body? Were you allowed or encouraged to fight back physically? Were you comforted and protected? Did you learn to run away? Or to stand stoically in the face of teasing or abuse? Or did you give up the choice of physical safety in order to survive?

Journal Questions: Body Identity

- How did you learn to live in your particular body during adolescence?
- How did you take care of your emerging body identity?
- What are your memories about confronting authority figures?

Conflicting Images

Vashti's story contains conflicting images. On the surface she lost her battle for choice and was punished by losing her place in the kingdom. Underneath, however, Vashti embodied the possibility of choosing against male control. Her story therefore contains an important image for women.

The tale of Vashti's refusal is set like a myth or folktale: after *seven* days of drinking and revelry, *seven* eunuchs summon Vashti and, after her refusal, there are *seven* counselors to guide the king. The numbers are part of a form that is typical of many fairytales, and the form suggests oral telling and re-telling. Such a myth often carries some general truth or folk-wisdom beyond its literal meaning, embedded in the process of the story. On one level, Vashti's story conveys the message that a woman who refused an order by her master would be banished from protection into a lawless world. On a deeper level, Vashti's story carries permission for women to protect their own bodies.

Vashti awakened the truth that women are simply different from men, not superior or inferior. Her identity rested on the ability to choose against the king's control, even though the consequence was probably death. She did not wait to be granted the right of choice; she took it. She faced the horror of being wiped off the history books, and yet her story lives in the celebration of Purim, outlasting even the historical records of King Xerxes in our collective memory.

As we work with the story of Vashti and bring our own lives to her drama, we can begin with her decision to choose against the dominant value system. Vashti's impulsive assertion of her right to choose is part of God's Biblical story, handed down through Jewish history and the canon of Scripture that we inherited.

We grow up with those same conflicting images, of obedience and independence. Although little girls are encouraged from birth to "be nice" and act more cooperatively than boys, strong role differences do not surface until puberty. The independence of Vashti's choice may be carried under the surface by images and stories, until a woman is strong enough or desperate enough to assert her equal right as a human being to choose the boundaries of her selfhood.

Nobody ever talked to me about the doors in our culture that closed because I happened to be female. I was bombarded with the contemporary images of being female which put emphasis on make-up, clothes and behavior that would attract men. As my body developed sexually and I conformed as much as I could to those external images, my adventurous, androgynous self submerged and that part of my identity took on a mythic quality. At night, I starred in continued stories that sometimes went on for weeks, working out the possibilities of life, trying to make peace with my femaleness.

As I sought models for being a woman, the seeds of my nascent self came from the stories of endurance and practical accomplishments of Western pioneer women. My own sense of identity as a female came from my Dutch grandmother. She influenced me both directly and indirectly. I lived with her until I was six, and she was a regular part of our family life until I went off to college. Her body and her personality made a strong impression on me. She also lived in my father's stories and his own value system.

There is little written record of my grandmother's life, except for dates in the family Bible, but I have some of her kitchen utensils and they remind me of who she was. One of the utensils is a funny wooden spoon, all worn down on one side, that she used for making cookie dough. That spoon contains all the sounds and smells and warmth of her welcome kitchen. Grandmother Zoet was full of energy. She kept three houses painted and shingled for renters, she nursed people in a town with no doctor, and she could always find a bit of fur or silk to make a plain hat celebrative. Although she lived a hearty "Yes" to the cultural role for women in her Dutch community, she also said "No" to being a compliant underling.

For me, the problem with my grandmother's model was that it was essentially neutered. Since she was fifty-four when I was born, she was long past her "feminine" period of trying to be sexually attractive to men. She was fully coherent as a woman by the time I knew her. Thus, her life gave me a picture of my own working self in the world, but no place for my sexuality.

Gradually, without conscious decision, I developed two stories of my future and never examined how they *didn't* fit together. In one scenario I finished college, married a professional man and settled in a college town like the one in which I grew up, repeating the life of my mother. This scenario took on reality as I began to date and feel the sexual excitement of being attractive to men. This story-line fit my cultural image of being female.

In the other scenario I remained single, went to graduate school and became a judge dealing with settlements of human disputes. This second image had earlier roots in the androgynous period of my childhood, from the days of living with my grandmother. This story-line fit my inner image of myself as an autonomous and self-sufficient person. This was my soul image.

When I married at twenty-two, I felt as chosen and special as Vashti must have felt when she became the queen. But, I began living a crazy mixture of my two story-lines. I put aside my real vocational ambitions in favor of being an Army wife, and I traded my strong sexual feelings for some neutralized image of being "a wife." I carried my nascent ego identity in the spiritual stream, because there was no way to develop the other two streams fully. I felt most alive when I was playing the piano, teaching creatively, or writing short stories.

Journal Questions:
Conflicting Images

- As a young adult, what were the activities that kept alive your sense of self?

- How does/did marriage affect your picture?

- What other images and/or relationships are suggested by your memories of choosing your own path in life?

Conclusion

When Vashti said "No!" to the cultural expectations of her world, she said "Yes!" to the beginnings of her self. Every two-year-old does the same thing within the context of their family. Every adult must repeat the same assertion within the context of their larger community. Vashti established a nascent self within her culture by making a choice that was available to males, but not to females.

Although Vashti's name was eliminated from official court records, her spirit lives on in the story of Esther. Her choice actually meant spiritual survival at the very point when her physical life was jeopardized. Confronting the threat of violence, which her culture used to keep women "in line," gave dimension to her character, gave her a body and a name and a story with which we can identify. Vashti embodied a personal self against the cultural images of the king.

4. SPIRITUAL HERITAGE

A Larger Context for Life

A mentor is one who thinks, remembers and teaches another. Mordecai, Esther's cousin and father by adoption, tutored Esther's inner self by linking her with God through the religious heritage of the Jewish people. Her heritage gave her a spiritual context for understanding who she was and why she was alive. As a mentor, Mordecai extended the cultural range of possibilities for Esther to include relationship with the living God. This relationship meant opening to the mystery of a spiritual reality manifested in the physical world.

Connecting with Community

In order to understand Esther's spiritual heritage, we need to begin with knowledge of her people: she was born a Jew. The Jews had a long history of valuing and celebrating family life. Although Jewish society was patriarchal, their traditional stories included women in roles of authority. The primary fact of their existence was their covenant relationship with God, who called out prophets and judges to guide them. When Jerusalem was destroyed in 587 B.C. and the people were deported to Babylon, the center of worship shifted away from the Temple.

Jews were scattered in small communities throughout the Babylonian empire, and worship was centered around telling and re-telling the stories of God and the promise of God's continuing relationship with Israel. For the Jews this was a message of unfolding revelation and continuing creation, not just reverence for something that happened in the ancient past. Through the psalms and wisdom writings, as well as the Torah, Jews-in-exile maintained their identity as the people of God even though they were scattered. Their faith also allowed them to be realistic about their present difficulties.

As a Jew, then, Esther was born to a story of relationship with God that connected her with past and future, with the essential goodness and promise of life. The death of Esther's parents can be understood within the larger context of Jewish history, because life and death was assumed to have a larger purpose than individual existence. While the Jews interpreted the Babylonian exile as a time of punishment for their unfaithfulness, they also hoped for a better future through their renewed response to God's guidance.

Just as for the Jews, our ethnic and religious communities give us an intermediate context for our lives, a context between individual and the national collective levels. Our spiritual heritage is an important source of affirmation and sense of belonging to something larger than individual life. This may either be liberating or repressive for women, but in either case, spiritual heritage provides a framework for values that connect us with past and future. If we are going to choose some kind of new pattern, then our family values, stories and rituals become part of the change process.

My external values have come most clearly from my father's side of the family. The Zoets and Zylstras were Dutch immigrants who came from the Friesian part of Holland in the late nineteenth century. They were hardworking and thrifty Calvinists, lured by the promise of fertile land. They understood their journey to America in Mosaic terms as a journey under covenant protection (and stern judgment) of God. Women were expected to obey the patriarchal men without question, but conditions in this country required teamwork and cooperation. The pioneer mentality of my Dutch heritage has been helpful to me, as Peter and I have moved from place to place with the Army for the past twenty years.

My internal spiritual stream can be traced to my mother's side of the family. The McLaurins came to Mississippi from Scotland around 1800. My mother's Scottish Presbyterian background gave me a love for books and music. Tuberculosis stalked her side of the family, and it has haunted my mother's sense of her own body. Perhaps the specter of death stimulated my own questions about life and death as a teenager. Mother's church background prevailed when we moved from the Dutch community in Lynden to Bellingham, Washington, and I joined the Presbyterian church when I turned twelve.

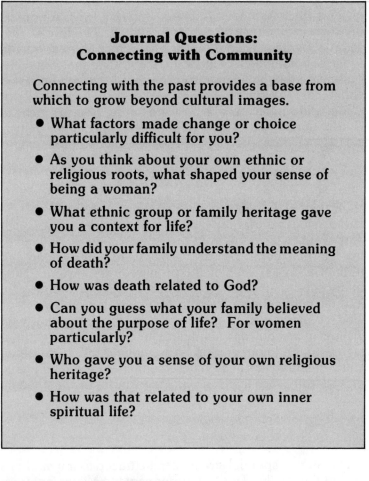

**Journal Questions:
Connecting with Community**

Connecting with the past provides a base from which to grow beyond cultural images.

- What factors made change or choice particularly difficult for you?

- As you think about your own ethnic or religious roots, what shaped your sense of being a woman?

- What ethnic group or family heritage gave you a context for life?

- How did your family understand the meaning of death?

- How was death related to God?

- Can you guess what your family believed about the purpose of life? For women particularly?

- Who gave you a sense of your own religious heritage?

- How was that related to your own inner spiritual life?

Connecting Two Worlds

Mordecai helped Esther to develop in two different cultures—the Persian court and the Hebrew community. He was an ideal mentor because he gave Esther a larger context for her life than the king's culture. Mordecai helped her identify her strengths, and yet he gave her a basic sense of values that went beyond her looks. She learned to value her religious heritage as an experience of community and support before she left home for the harem of King Xerxes.

Mordecai himself stood with one foot in the Jewish community of Susa and one foot in the court. Archeological findings indicate that the court at Susa was magnificent with art and architecture. Culture life must have been exciting and varied as well. Mordecai had chosen to stay in Susa when other Jews went back to Jerusalem. A third-generation exile from Israel, Mordecai was a city-man acquainted with court politics. He had spotted intrigue against the king and had the connections to see that the perpetrators were successfully prosecuted.

When Vashti was banished, it was Mordecai who brought Esther to the competition for a new queen. He affirmed her beauty, along with her spiritual heritage. Mordecai recognized Esther's attractiveness and schooled her in how to operate through that advantage, not to be trapped by it! He reflected to Esther a part of her strength and self-identity, but not the whole story. Mordecai's own ambitions were a bridge for Esther to move beyond her own Jewish community.

Mordecai cared more about the opportunity for Esther to be in court than he did about Jewish separateness. The issue of sexual purity among the Jews had been a problem since Jerusalem was destroyed and the Hebrews were deported to Babylon, nearly a hundred years before the reign of King Xerxes. Mordecai's apparent opportunism on this point contrasts sharply with his piety in refusing to bow to Haman. However, Mordecai's ability to function in two worlds, two cultures, two value-systems, made him an ideal mentor for Esther. He could help her bridge the limitations of her own cultural stereotypes.

He understood how different Jewish monotheism was from the prevailing norms of the Persian court. When Esther was chosen to enter the court, Mordecai cautioned her not to reveal her Jewish identity. Since the public worship life of the Jews was carried on by the men, Mordecai's restriction would not have prevented Esther from praying to God in private. His admonition to keep her Jewish identity secret did mean she could not practice some of the dietary rules of Judaism. He was alert to the dangers and opportunities of court life, and he had given her enough training as a Jew to make it dangerous for her.

From Mordecai, Esther took basic supplies for her spiritual journey, but she had to travel the way herself. Symbolically, she embarked upon a heroic journey, leaving her own people and the limitations of her culture, for the highest prize in the kingdom. It was a classic heroic quest!

A mentor like Mordecai is hard for women in our culture to find. A parent is usually too enmeshed in one's childhood cultural setting to provide that bridging function. An interested and experienced "third party" may often be found in educational or work settings, but the traditional woman who marries and stays at home is isolated from most mentoring possibilities.

Even in the right setting, it is difficult for women to find a mentor. Perhaps men expect women to fulfill traditional roles, so potential mentors simply do not see vocational possibilities for women that they would see in equally talented men. At this time, there are not many older women in public roles to be mentors for women. However, women are moving toward each other in work settings to begin the process of networking as a variation of mentoring.

A mentor is more than a role-model. A mentor calls forth unique gifts in someone else by living out of their own gifts fully and freely. Our cultural image keeps an admired person at a distance or on a pedestal, like a silhouette that requires adjustment for the proper fit. A mentor encourages uniqueness, instead of fitting a mold, by being centered in her own gifts *and* committed to the relationship for mutual spiritual growth.

My own experience with mentors has been both frightening and positive. Out of my own willingness to walk where I did not know the way, several mentors have helped me make important transitions. I remember a college professor who read aloud my paper on T.S. Eliot as an example of what *not* to do, and then said, "Miss Zoet, this is too poor for me to grade, but I will work with you this year so you can learn what to look for." As we worked together, I began to understand what it meant to be in dialogue with a poem and its author.

He literally taught me the skills of reading and writing that I needed to survive at Harvard.

Twenty years later, another mentor told me he was saving what I wrote "because you'll want to publish this someday." He blessed my writing when I did not have enough faith to believe in it myself. At the time, I valued my creative spontaneity and adaptability, but he saw possibilities for my skills in a larger context.

Elizabeth O'Connor, author of many books about Church of the Saviour,* calls every Christian to be a "patron of gifts." A patron or mentor helps to name and bless the nascent spiritual identity of each person into being. In her book *Eighth Day of Creation,* O'Connor writes, "Churches are endangered because they do not know the necessity of [patrons] for the emergence of gifts and flow of creativity."** As a member of Church of the Saviour, I have been blessed and encouraged by many members of that church community who take mentoring seriously.

Journal Questions:
Connecting Two Worlds

- At some critical point in your life, can you identify a mentor who helped you bridge a cultural or vocational chasm?

- Who was it? How did you know each other? How did the bridging happen? What has happened to your relationship since then?

- How did your parents feel about your mentors?

- Can you identify some of the difficulties with the mixture of parent and mentor?

---

*Church of the Saviour, Washington, D.C.
**Elizabeth O'Connor, *Eighth Day of Creation: Gifts and Creativity,* pp. 34-35.

Connecting with Dreams

Mordecai had another kind of influence in Esther's life: he had a mystical side to complement his political acumen and leadership in the Jewish community. Mordecai's attention to his own dreams encouraged Esther's spiritual development and her openness to something beyond the laws of their religious background.

In the fuller Greek text the Book of Esther begins with a terrifying dream. The dream suggests the chaos of creation from Genesis or the terror of Israel trapped between the Red Sea and Pharoah's troops. It pictures a prophetic role for someone out of the people threatened with extinction.

MORDECAI'S DREAM

Shrieks and cries in the darkness
Earth trembles and cracks
Chaos coils, explodes
Smoke suffocates
Terror chokes

Dragons battle
Two snouts aflame
Talons tearing
Flesh hangs ragged
Snarling rage

Death swirls

A tiny cry
Wrenched from rock
Reaches for life

Death stalks

Cry turns to tear
Droplets form
A stream

Spring
Springing out
Swelling
River
Flooding

Dawn then
Sun...light...help

The humble rise
To devour the mighty!

Mordecai's nightmare set the drama of Esther's story within a clash of two cultures. In the dream two dragons make war and threaten destruction to all within range. Only the cry brings relief. The cry has no force of its own, but the sound brings forth response; droplets converge until a mighty river forms. The cry creates, as though connected with a mysterious force just waiting to raise up the humble and bring down the mighty.

Mordecai puzzled about his dream because he did not yet understand it, but he did assume it had meaning for him. Mordecai's belief structure included belief in guidance from God through dreams and visions. Mordecai knew the story of a dream preceding God's covenant with Abraham (Gen. 15); the story of Joseph's dream of sheaves bowing down which set in motion the movement of the Jews to Egypt (Gen. 37); and the story of God's promise to Jacob as he returned to the land of his fathers (Gen. 28). He knew that God had revealed guidance for the Jews through dreams.

The history of God's deliverance was particularly important to Jews during the period after Jerusalem fell: it kept alive their hope of being reunited once again at some time in the future. From his own place in the Persian court at Susa,

Mordecai could have answered the question, "Who am I?" with a clear reply: "I am a Jew, part of God's revelation in this time and place."

As women in a materialistic culture, we have grown up with little regard for dreams. However, our Biblical heritage encourages attention to dreams. We can come to Mordecai's dream with a sense of wonder and expectation, just as he did.

Could it be true that there is a force in the universe wanting to coalesce from our cries and tears? When we come to the end of human power to oppose destructive forces like the dragons of war, can we believe that a cry against injustice will set in motion a redemptive stream? Is the concept of a force waiting, wanting, another way to talk about the power of God or the meaning of Jesus? Consider that possibility in the light of history for women.

For me, dragons conjure stories of knights in armor and ladies in castles. At this fairy-tale level, it is difficult to take Mordecai's dream seriously as a part of my own spiritual path. But when I make the effort to imagine myself as the dragons, fighting destructively to the death, I can hear the conflicting power struggles going on inside and outside of me.

As I let my consciousness move through the tangible reality of this book, this chair, this time of day, reaching out with my spirit into the dream of Mordecai, I am not in the present at all. I am in some other time frame.

The dragons in my life right now are clearly vocational and sexual. One stomps and tears at my commitment to write this book, critical of every idea, flaming with cultural demands for facts and studies and footnotes. The other laughs in vicious mockery at my pretentions of having something to say to other women.

My soul is a tiny spring, hardly more than a trickle of water. I want very much to feel the pouring strength and aliveness of becoming a stream and then a mighty river, but for right now, I am caught between the dragons! I feel little, powerless, crying out to God for a way to find meaning beyond my own household.

Then other images come: fears of the future, of war, of hunger, of illness and senility in an uncaring place. I feel the ground tremble as the dragons of our culture heave and pant above me. I am below, in the earth, waiting to be born. As they stomp and tear, the surface cracks and a tiny trickle of water begins...cool, clear water glinting diamond in the early morning dawn. I see women with caring eyes and out-stretched hands, beckoning, inviting me to flow with them between the dragons.

I know that these images carry truth for me. I draw the images in my journal and return to the dream again and again, as a source of energy when I feel helpless. The image of a stream breaking out of a cry is full of wonder for me.

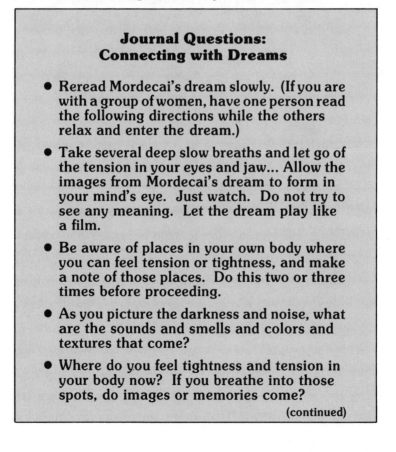

Journal Questions:
Connecting with Dreams

- Reread Mordecai's dream slowly. (If you are with a group of women, have one person read the following directions while the others relax and enter the dream.)

- Take several deep slow breaths and let go of the tension in your eyes and jaw... Allow the images from Mordecai's dream to form in your mind's eye. Just watch. Do not try to see any meaning. Let the dream play like a film.

- Be aware of places in your own body where you can feel tension or tightness, and make a note of those places. Do this two or three times before proceeding.

- As you picture the darkness and noise, what are the sounds and smells and colors and textures that come?

- Where do you feel tightness and tension in your body now? If you breathe into those spots, do images or memories come?

(continued)

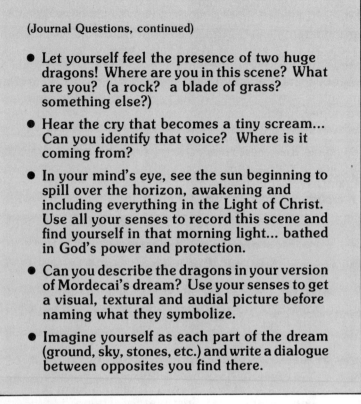

(Journal Questions, continued)

- Let yourself feel the presence of two huge dragons! Where are you in this scene? What are you? (a rock? a blade of grass? something else?)

- Hear the cry that becomes a tiny scream... Can you identify that voice? Where is it coming from?

- In your mind's eye, see the sun beginning to spill over the horizon, awakening and including everything in the Light of Christ. Use all your senses to record this scene and find yourself in that morning light... bathed in God's power and protection.

- Can you describe the dragons in your version of Mordecai's dream? Use your senses to get a visual, textural and audial picture before naming what they symbolize.

- Imagine yourself as each part of the dream (ground, sky, stones, etc.) and write a dialogue between opposites you find there.

Opening to Mystery

Mordecai's dream was a message of hope from God. It revealed the mystery of God *coming toward* the Hebrews, instead of the more common picture that humans had to propitiate many gods with sacrifices. Even though Mordecai did not understand the particular images at first, the dream contained the essence of Jewish faith: God would never abandon the Jews as a people.

The monotheistic covenant relationship between the Hebrews and God set the Jews apart from other ancient religions. Stories of Sarah and Abraham, Miriam and Moses, portrayed an intimate and personal relationship with the very principle of life: "I am that I am" was the name God

revealed to Moses (Ex 3:14). The covenant promise between God and the Hebrews was nothing less than a promise
of spiritual identity for all Jews.

Mordecai believed that God would not abandon the Jews,
even though external signs of God's protection seemed faint
during the exile period. Mordecai accepted the traditional
belief that God acted through people and nature in order to
guide the Jews. There was no separation between physical
and spiritual reality for the Hebrews.

Twentieth-century Americans tend to separate physical
and spiritual matters. Simply by having different words for
"spirit" and "body," we split Hebrew understanding into
tangible and invisible categories. Our cultural understanding,
based on Newtonian physics and the scientific materialism of
the past three centuries, discounts the importance of dreams
and faith in God.

In this century there has been renewed interest in the
unseen forces that permeate physical reality. Einstein
postulated matter and energy as different forms of whatever
atoms are. Jung explored the language of dream images
across cultural boundaries to discover a common source. He
called for increased awareness of "the Feminine" or regard
for intuitive ways of knowing. John Sanford and Morton
Kelsey, each an Episcopal priest and Jungian analyst, have
written extensively about the link between Biblical faith and
dream imagery. Brain researchers are beginning to explore
right brain capacities for non-linear thinking, while physicists
explore the possibility that we live in a conscious universe.
Modern science is bringing us back to the mystery that
Mordecai approached from his own understanding of God
and the purpose of being God's covenant people.[*]

------

*For additional reading on this subject, I recommend the following books:
    C.G. Jung, *Memories, Dreams and Reflections*
    John Sanford, *Dreams, God's Forgotten Language*
    Morton Kelsey, *The Other Side of Silence*
    Jacob Needleman, *Sense of the Cosmos*

While modern science is revealing more and more signs that the universe is a living organism, endlessly and mysteriously interconnected, theology is beginning to move from a series of static propositions *about* God, to metaphors and parables conveying an unfolding relationship with God.* We are living in an exciting breakthrough period between science and religion. Our culture, through the streams of science and feminism, is beginning to open to the mystery of a living universe. Women may well be the channel through which these separate cultural streams converge most clearly.

For me, opening to the mystery of living *in* God (rather than the more traditional view that God's Spirit is alive in me) came more out of music than the language of the church. As a teenager, I practiced the pipe organ in a mortuary (because the church was kept too cold in winter), and there I had a chance to experience the mystery of death without the personal trauma of losing a loved one. I began to ponder my beliefs about death as I practiced the chorales of Bach, many of which had texts about death and resurrection. I was enormously curious about the dead people who shared that quiet sanctuary with me. "What really happens when somebody dies?" I wondered.

It was clear to me that something important was gone! These people were different from sleeping people. Their *aliveness* was gone. I knew that aliveness had once been there, allowing these same people to grow and change over time. Now that development was stopped (although the natural process of decay and change would continue). Out of that experience, I began my spiritual quest with the proposition that *God is the aliveness in all things and all things are connected in the aliveness of God.*

Because I was not embarrassed to be staring at these people who could not look back at me, I had time to absorb the infinite variations among them. Each one was different, and I was struck by the mystery of how new things come into being. *"Are these people a growing edge of God?"* I asked myself, *"and am I too?"*

---

*Sallie McFague, *Metaphorical Theology*.

The language I heard at St. James Presbyterian Church in Bellingham, Washington, was not the language of my questions in the mortuary. In fact I do not remember much that I heard in church during my teenage years. The language of creeds and confessions seemed to answer questions I was *not* asking, and Biblical exegesis did not explain the question of death that I *was* pondering.

My parents took their faith seriously, and I understood that my father felt some spiritual connection to his medical practice, though it often took him away from time with his family. I never questioned the need for serving the wounded or giving to the poor, but I wanted to know more about God and why people had to die.

Are we the growing edge of God? Somehow that question made death explainable to me. All living things had to die, I knew, because that was part of the natural cycle of any organism.

I didn't know then that I was asking a theological question, but I know that now. My question continues to be a guide for me as I read and study, make pottery and cook dinner, reflect and write: Are we the growing edge of God? If the answer is "Yes," then that has enormous implications for how we live with each other and with the rest of creation.

In retrospect I see that I grew up with two different interpretations of "Who am I?" One came from my body and my mystical experience in the mortuary, and the other came from the language of the church and our culture.

Standing alone in the mortuary I was awed by the variety in human form and the finality of death: all were equal there. I learned to love my own aliveness and to believe in my worth as a child of God. Until adolescence, I got the same message of worth from the church, but at puberty I began to experience difference and segregation because I was female. The message I got from the church was that women were different and inferior. The minister laughed at my expressed desire to be a minister. I heard the creation story from Genesis, chapter two, in which women were blamed for separating humans from God. Nobody preached about the other creation story in the first chapter of Genesis, in which God's image was fully expressed by the wholeness of male and female together. I understood that, according to the church, being female meant being bad. That understanding felt different from my previous understanding of being a beloved child of God.

My own sense of God fell silent during those years, because the adults in church could think more logically and theologically than I could. But my spiritual stream was open to the mystery of God, and I knew somewhere deep in my body that I was still a child of God. The question for me became, "How can I become an *adult* of God?"

Have you experienced the mystery of God's presence? Was that experience connected with your experience of church? And was it related in any way to the messages you got from the church about being female? As you consider your own spiritual development, allow nonverbal experiences, such as music and art, to be part of the stream, too.

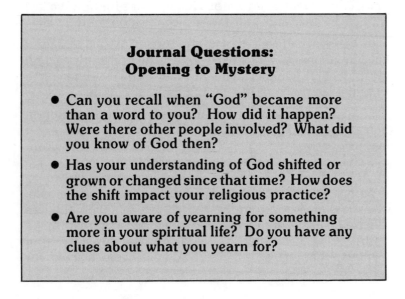

Journal Questions:
Opening to Mystery

- Can you recall when "God" became more than a word to you? How did it happen? Were there other people involved? What did you know of God then?

- Has your understanding of God shifted or grown or changed since that time? How does the shift impact your religious practice?

- Are you aware of yearning for something more in your spiritual life? Do you have any clues about what you yearn for?

Conclusion

The spiritual heritage which Mordecai gave to Esther freed her from bondage to the cultural constraints on women. Connecting with her religious community gave Esther a sense of belonging to history and to the stories of God's covenant relationship with the Jews. Mordecai's own skill in bridging the gap between two cultures gave Esther a mentor that many of us must seek outside of home. Further, Mordecai exposed Esther to his own mystical understanding of God at work through dreams, which later gave her a way to understand God's spiritual reality in the bodily decision she had to make. Mordecai not only affirmed an alternate reality for Esther, but he also gave her specific ways to move from where she was in the culture to the open mystery of God's continuing presence in all things.

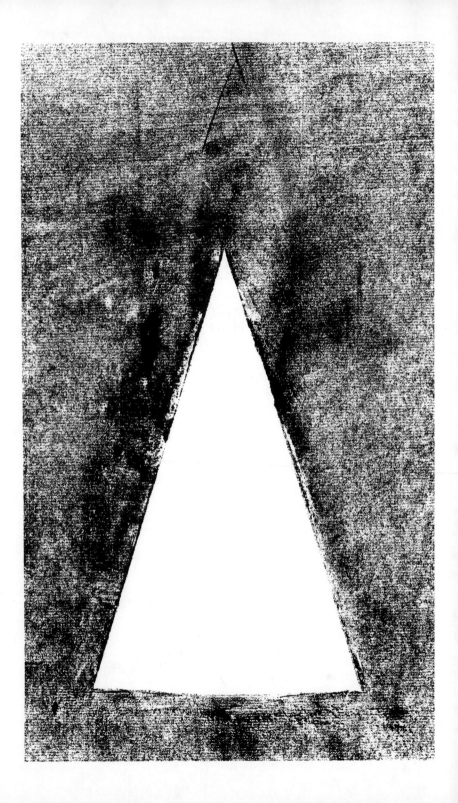

5. SEXUAL IDENTITY
Internal Images of Being Female

A woman must come to some understanding of her gender identity from inside her body, as well as interpreting her life as a female through the reactions of others. Internal body awareness is stimulated by people and things in the environment, but it grows from a sensory base inside one's skin. Hegai's role was to awaken Esther's senses and connect her sensuality with cultural images of her sexuality.

Our body awareness begins with our parents. Every woman has had two parents, whether they were actually known or not. Because parents influence us before we have developed conscious language to understand or interpret events, parents shape our lives from inside and outside. As adults, in order to separate from the unconscious messages we carry about what it means to be female, we need to be "orphaned" figuratively or literally.

Hegai's Influence

Hegai, head of the king's harem, was the guard and guide of all the beautiful young virgins who were brought to him before going to the king's bed. He had seen all types and sizes, from peasants to aristocrats. In the year they spent under his care and direction, he awakened their bodies with oil and spices and taught them many varieties of sexual pleasure, so the king could experience newness and glory in his own prowess. The king's sexual prowess symbolized fertility for the whole kingdom, and it was Hegai's role to prepare all the young virgins to be suitable partners for the king. Hegai was a connoisseur of bodily pleasure. Hegai could give the kind of training no mother could provide!

Hegai was a eunuch, neutered so the king could be sure he alone had "first rites." In a culture where fertility was a sign of power and wealth, Hegai was stripped of his own sexual power, and so he was dependent upon the king's hierarchical system for a place of value. As a guide for Esther during the period between Mordecai's fatherly protection and her sexual initiation with the king, Hegai's job was to sharpen Esther's sexual identity as a female within the Persian cultural norms.

In contrast to Mordecai, Hegai was not there to substitute for Esther's parents, nor was he interested in her full development as a human being. He was not even concerned about her fuller identity as a bearer of children. His only job was to prepare her to be the king's sexual partner. If she conceived, there were others to worry about raising any children.

Good parents in our culture, with its puritanical strain, often do not emphasize body pleasure and body-knowing. In fact, our culture encourages external images of being female to the point of denying the soul that is present and sacred as a part of one's body.

Our cultural myth associates sexuality with beauty in young females. A fairy-tale we have all watched and read is that a beautiful woman will be chosen by the perfect man and live happily ever after. Even though we are not so naive about "happily ever after" any more, most of us want the access to money and power that beauty brings. The power in Esther's beauty was dependent upon selection. We live in a similar public value system. If someone else holds the power to provide what we want, or we think another person has that power, then we may live into the image of what it means to be female, which is signaled by that other person's reaction. Someone who holds a stereotyped image of what it means to be a successful female is not being a mentor, a "patron of gifts!"

Living into someone else's picture of who we ought to be makes us eager consumers of diets, beauty preparations and clothes. There is real economic gain and manipulative power in making women feel "unbeautiful" and dependent upon male approval. As long as we evaluate our lives from the standpoint of a critical onlooker, we will be cooperative consumers and compliant receivers. If we see ourselves against the perfect female ideal and fall short (or fat or old, etc.), we stay subservient consumers, economic commodities and unpaid labor in an exploitive system.

Stereotyped sexuality masquerades as intimacy in our culture, and the darker side of that masquerade is sexual abuse. Whenever we separate sensory stimulation from the larger issue of spiritual growth, the danger of objectifying ourselves or others is very real.

If we do recognize that being female is only one stream of our development—one aspect of a more complex life—then we can explore the internal sensory experience of our own sexuality with gladness and curiosity.

It never occurred to me in adolescence, when I was splitting the image of my sexuality from my spiritual body-awareness, that the aliveness I felt inside could be my own sexuality. Because the words associated with sexual differences between men and women did not describe my internal feelings, I assumed that I was wrong! I knew that I did not fit the norms I saw in *Seventeen* magazine. My short curly hair and athletic interests separated me from the "Junior Miss" types, while my academic ambitions set me apart from the dreamy teenage dating scene.

My daydreams had less to do with finding a man who would do something to me or for me, than with discovering positive stories of being female. As a pre-adolescent, I often made up stories in which I was the main character. Frequently, I pictured myself as an Indian woman, alone, independent, able to live freely in nature. As a Campfire Girl, I chose "Sacajewea" as my name, and I loved to read about her courage and ingenuity as the guide for Lewis and Clark. Her stories were full of sensory images: fires and starry nights, buckskin dresses and furs, bird-songs and horses. She embodied a sensual, earthy, self-sufficient woman whom I recognized as part of my sexual self. I know that she represents unclaimed parts of myself even now. In Jungian terms, she is my shadow self. That Indian woman carried my sensory awareness until a later time, when my body was ready to receive the external images of sexuality and integrate them.

There was also a teenaged "Hegai" in my life, a man who blessed my nascent sexuality. We "went steady" for a year until he started pressing for marriage and I got scared. I was lucky or wise or protected by my own feelings of fear, because by the time I finished college, he had married and abused two wives.

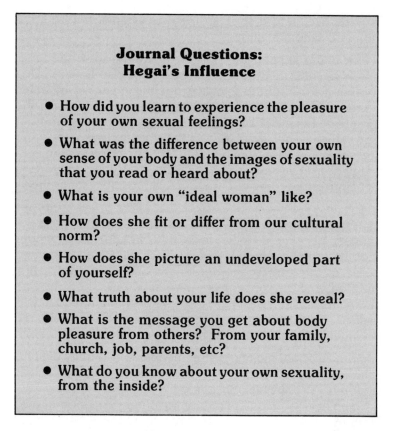

**Journal Questions:
Hegai's Influence**

- How did you learn to experience the pleasure of your own sexual feelings?

- What was the difference between your own sense of your body and the images of sexuality that you read or heard about?

- What is your own "ideal woman" like?

- How does she fit or differ from our cultural norm?

- How does she picture an undeveloped part of yourself?

- What truth about your life does she reveal?

- What is the message you get about body pleasure from others? From your family, church, job, parents, etc?

- What do you know about your own sexuality, from the inside?

Messages from Mother

Esther was orphaned sometime in childhood. Mordecai provided guidance and protection for her as she grew up, and then she entered an all-female society in the king's harem. She may have learned as much about her own body from being with the women as she did from Hegai.

In some way every child is awakened to her bodyness by her mother. Before there is language to name feelings, a mother's touch conveys how much safety and love is available for the child. During adolescence, many of those early pre-verbal body-memories are recycled by sexual touch. In a sense every child needs to be "orphaned" from her mother, before she can truly experience her own full range of sexual feelings.

For many women the task of separating from the inner image of mother is difficult, because we also have a living mother who continues to live out the meaning of being female at some level. The task is further complicated if she did not do the inner work of separating from her own mother and father. Then we received the unconscious needs and fears that she carried in her own body with the very milk of babyhood. If we have some guilt about rejecting her portrait of being female, then our primary relationship with mother is even more complicated.

"We all marry to find a good mother," someone has said. Indeed, we may also marry to solidify our adolescent gender identity. I have a hunch that my husband Peter awakened some of my earliest mother-longings when we were first married, and I suffered from periodic depressions the first few years of our marriage. Now I suspect that my body was registering the fact that Peter would not complete my spiritual journey for me. I would have to do it alone, later.

Some women never develop their female identity beyond childhood dependence, even though they themselves bear children. "You're still my little girl" is a phrase many grown women hear from one parent or the other. The mother who does not do her own inner work of integrating at midlife may try to live through her daughter, experiencing the same dead-end to her own sexual development by repeating the adolescent splitting between sexuality and spiritual body-awareness over and over.

Other women never make the transit from Motherhood to Womanhood, because they continue to identify with their own mothers and never fill out the other strands of self. Their development stays at the level of mothering without bringing in the streams of spiritual and vocational wholeness.

There are some women who do succeed in expanding the role of mother to express the fullness of womanhood. Recently, I read a story* about Hale House in New York City,

---

*Washington *Post,* Sunday, November 18, 1984.

where a seventy-nine year-old woman provides care for babies born to drug-addicted mothers. These babies are born with their own withdrawal symptoms, often complicated by other physical difficulties. Mother Hale has been licensed by the city and was recently honored for her many years of providing a home for countless youngsters from that neighborhood. She has expanded her female identity to include the spiritual and vocational streams.

My own mother did not have that kind of strong maternal identity. In one way it made my task of separating easier. In another, it made her influence harder to identify. She often said to me, "You're just like your father," and I believed her. Now I see more of my connections with her. So much of her power and influence was nonverbal, going back to very early life experiences. I could not find the words to think of our likeness, because at the time of our bonding, I did not have language to store those memories. Now, through deep relaxation and guided imagery, I have become aware of many unconscious body ties with her.

Adolescence was a time of struggle between my own body's femaleness and my mother's version of being female. I wanted to be attractive, to know about clothes and sex and feeling good about my body. My mother did not seem interested in any of those things. Without any community rituals that would legitimatize my questions, I did not feel free to find other women who might teach me about those things either, so I furtively read movie magazines at the drugstore and experimented with makeup at slumber parties.

I left for college, determined not to follow my mother's path into the drudgery of mothering. I felt her anger and despair, her conflict between unrealized dreams and the sacrifice of her choice to marry and have children. When the conflict between dreams and sacrifice got too much for her, she always got sick. I didn't want to live that way, and yet I didn't know how to claim my soul a different way.

Like Esther, I left home and "was adopted," though my external leave-taking came through marriage into another family system. Marriage did *not* do the inner work of separating from my mother, although I thought it did at the time. Unconsciously I drew the curtains down around my sexuality and neutralized my energies to be the partner to Peter that fit my mother's image of marriage. On the surface I related well to both men and women. Inside, I felt detached from my body, strangely neutral as a woman and still waiting to wake up.

I know that my *interpretation* of mother's image of marriage was probably not the image she actually had. It has taken me a long time to learn that! Furthermore, I suspect her picture has changed over the years. She married to have children and enjoy the companionship that our cultural myth promises in marriage. Her own body rejection was so deep that she did not find a way to let the braided stream of her early adult years converge fully.

My adult life has been something of a mirror reflection of hers: I worked hard on my vocational identity in the world and did not have any children, so I missed the body experience that my mother explored through childbirth. By choosing an opposite stream in reaction to her stream, I have been just as deeply connected to her as someone who chose to *duplicate* her mother's pattern. Now, I am able to celebrate the mystical-imaginative-spiritual stream that my mother and I did share as I grew up, and I can explore mothering in other ways.

In reflecting on my mother's life and what she modeled for me about being a woman in our culture, I have to start with the differences and similarities in our bodies. Then, I have to remember the difference between her time and mine and take into account the information now available to me. And then I can give thanks for the choices she did make to love and care for me and my two younger sisters.

Most of all, I am beginning to see my mother as a separate person with limits and opportunities that were different from mine. I do give thanks for the gift of life itself that she gave me out of her own body's vital energy. Some of our most intimate conversations recently have been in answer to my questions about her life at the time of my birth. I realize that I started then to form my impressions of what it means to be a woman.

Our mothers do set the stage for splitting body awareness and adolescent sexuality. In early life the touch they give sets our pattern of safety (or distrust) which may be re-activated during early sexual experiences. Our mothers also influence whether or not we want to fit the cultural norms, depending on the circumstances of family life. Until we separate from the inner images that were set by our mothers, we cannot form an integrated sensory base for our own adult sexuality.

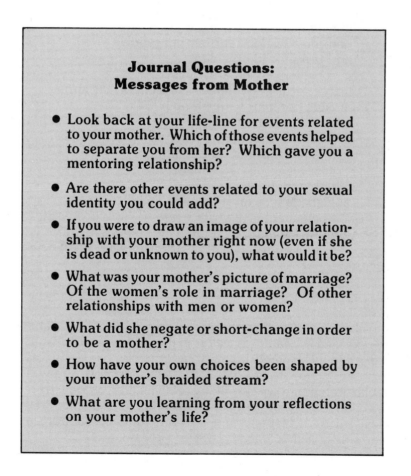

Journal Questions:
Messages from Mother

- Look back at your life-line for events related to your mother. Which of those events helped to separate you from her? Which gave you a mentoring relationship?

- Are there other events related to your sexual identity you could add?

- If you were to draw an image of your relationship with your mother right now (even if she is dead or unknown to you), what would it be?

- What was your mother's picture of marriage? Of the women's role in marriage? Of other relationships with men or women?

- What did she negate or short-change in order to be a mother?

- How have your own choices been shaped by your mother's braided stream?

- What are you learning from your reflections on your mother's life?

Messages from Father

Hegai's role of introducing Esther to the sensual pleasure of her own body in preparation for intercourse with the king necessarily built on messages from Esther's childhood about her identity as a female. Esther had neither mother nor father to provide a framework of values for being in the world as a female, but Mordecai linked Esther to her father's family. Hebrew literature praised the industrious wife and mother, giving Esther a clear picture of an ideal woman:

> She rises while it is yet night
> and provides food for her household
> and tasks for her maidens.
> She considers a field and buys it;
> with the fruit of her hands she plants a vineyard.
> She girds her loins with strength
> and makes her arms strong.
> She perceives that her merchandise is profitable.
> Her lamp does not go out at night...
>
> Strength and dignity are her clothing,
> and she laughs at the time to come.
> She opens her mouth with wisdom,
> and the teaching of kindness is on her tongue.
> (Proverbs 31, RSV)

Esther grew up within the Jewish community of Susa and she excelled in beauty, as well as in the wisdom and strength praised in this Hebrew poem from Proverbs. Since she was exposed to the Persian court through Mordecai, she was sophisticated and wise to that worldly culture as well. Her selection for the harem meant that Esther herself embodied ideals of both Hebrew and Persian womanhood from a man's perspective.

Although women have more legal rights today than in the time of Esther, most of us begin to define our sexual interaction with males through the response of a father, even one who is not physically present. Physically, even before we have the language to name what we feel, we learn to value or disrespect our bodies from the way our fathers react to us. How our fathers touch us and speak with us sets the framework for our ability to integrate cultural images with our body responses to men.

Spiritually, before we can know for ourselves, we also learn from our fathers whether or not females are considered to be fully human. Vocationally, our expectations for future work are set by our fathers' reactions to home and family. Our surnames are symbolic of the social identity that comes from our fathers' side. As the primary parent who models how a female can relate to males, our fathers are crucial.

Like Esther, I learned to interpret my life as a female through the language and responses of men, beginning with my father. He had shape and substance in the world. My father had the power to name me and thus to shape my sexuality.

Physically, my dad valued strength and energy, physical stamina and independent (though conservative) thinking. I am not aware that he noticed anybody sexually, except in a clinical sense. Since he was a family doctor, pregnancy was a matter of dinner-table discussion. Those discussions gave me an overwhelming sense of the responsibilities that could result from unbridled sexual feelings, without any sense of the joy or pleasure.

Spiritually, there was no doubt that my dad valued women, but he did not like any woman to challenge his hierarchical authority. As a "bossy" child at the table, the message I got was, "That will be enough, Grandmother!" When my dad said that, I knew he meant I was domineering, aggressive and that I did not understand my female (subservient) role. As I recall, I was usually trying to take charge of my two younger sisters. I learned to hate that "take charge" aspect of myself, because my father was so critical of it.

Vocationally, I did not get clear messages from my father. He respected practical women who were committed to the welfare of their children. He ridiculed the only female physician in town. Although he valued education, he honored native intelligence even more, and he encouraged me to use my own judgment in making decisions about work and money. He did not encourage me to seek a professional career, but he has been interested in how my pioneer values took shape within the framework of Peter's military career.

My father was strongly grounded in his own body; he liked to farm as a counter-balance to his medical practice. Working the land was his favorite form of recreation. He valued women (like his mother) who could work with his kind of stamina, and he honored handcrafts that women developed to relieve the cultural paucity of isolated communities. It's no surprise that I enjoy making pottery, my middle sister weaves and my youngest sister sews beautifully.

In fact, my father encouraged all three of his daughters to be strong, practical women who could work hard physically. He liked to be "on top and in charge," but he made it clear that we had the capacity for concentration and achievement. He raised all three of us to be good Hebrew wives, like the pattern described in the poem from Proverbs. He rejected the cultural norms of seductive beauty that we saw in magazines or on television.

During adolescence, your relationship with your father probably set the language and thought patterns for understanding your sexuality, but even prior to adolescence his values set patterns of expectation for your body in marriage and motherhood. While his influence is not as early, nor as nonverbal as your mother's, your father's attitudes about beauty and mothering still need to be sorted out from the inner sense of your self as a female.

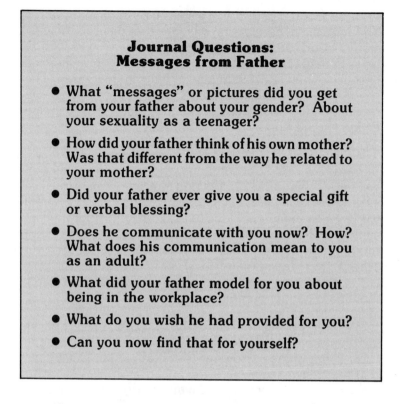

Journal Questions:
Messages from Father

- What "messages" or pictures did you get from your father about your gender? About your sexuality as a teenager?

- How did your father think of his own mother? Was that different from the way he related to your mother?

- Did your father ever give you a special gift or verbal blessing?

- Does he communicate with you now? How? What does his communication mean to you as an adult?

- What did your father model for you about being in the workplace?

- What do you wish he had provided for you?

- Can you now find that for yourself?

At Home in the Body

Hegai helped Esther clarify her sexual identity and grounded that identity in her physical body. When Esther entered the harem, she left the protective wing of Mordecai and stepped onto the stage of her own life, with the specific sexual guidance and encouragement of Hegai. If she was going to preserve the richness of her Hebrew background, Esther would have to do it herself.

As a teacher, Hegai brought a man's erotic attention to Esther without sexual intercourse. Hegai's responsibility was to bring our the fullest possible beauty of each virgin through a year-long program of sensual awakening. The women were schooled in every possible way that would please the king. It was the ultimate beauty spa!

Hegai favored Esther with a special position in the harem. She must have had special qualities that pleased the jaded connoisseur and piqued his interest in her future with the king. Perhaps Esther never was very detached from her body because of her Jewish heritage. Whatever the reason, when she finally went to the king's bed, it was Hegai who recommended that she go "unadorned." Hegai helped Esther "come home" to her own body.

We often search unsuccessfully for someone like Hegai in our modern world, for someone who will help us enjoy our sexuality "unadorned." Beyond the two-dimensional advertisement images of being female in our society, where do we learn to experience our full sexuality through the sensuality of our own bodies? Beyond the messages from mother and father, from the institutions of church and school, from friends (and foes), how can we learn to live "from the inside out?" How can we move from genital identity to gender identity?

We are missing the active body experiences between childhood and adulthood that came naturally to women in rural communities. Now we watch television. Everything gets sexualized and no act is too private to show. We are thus trained by our substitute media guides to look at our bodies from the outside, like a TV camera, and to fill any silence with sound lest we stumble upon the mystery of what our lives are for. "The pill" presumably makes intercourse a safe sport for everyone. Indeed, in our haste to "have it all," we seem to have lost the mystery of sexual intercourse to awaken a deeper level of sexuality.

In my own experience the question of choice has been critical to knowing my sexual identity "from the inside out." As a teenager, I distrusted my body, because "it" limited my activities, provoked wanted and unwanted attention from men, and carried the threat of pregnancy unless I "stood guard" over my feelings. Then, when I married, all the negative defensiveness was supposed to disappear in a mythical euphoria of sexual delight. In fact, I had never learned to trust the pleasure of my own sexual feelings.

As long as I regarded my body from an outsider's stand-point rather than my own, I could not really "be there" during intercourse. Gradually, I became conscious of choosing to be present or absent to my own body sensations. Learning that Peter and I could choose celibacy within marriage, and explore a range of intimacy that did not directly depend upon intercourse, has helped me to trust my own sensual self. I feel celibacy was a very useful choice for us for a limited period of time.

Other women may feel "at home" with their bodies and need to explore intentionally the spiritual or vocational streams, just as I have needed to connect my conscious self and my body-self. "Hegai" has come to my life in many different ways, each with a piece of experience through which I could discover the range of my own sensuality.

Your story will be different from mine, but I have a hunch that feeling detached from our bodies is quite a normal feeling for women in our culture. All of us have work to do integrating our body sexuality with the role of being female and being mothers, whether we actually have children or not.

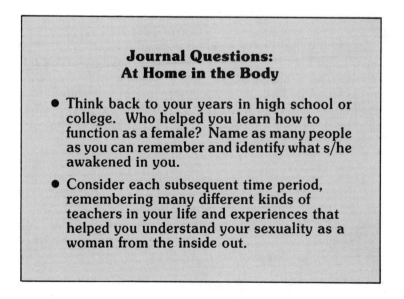

Journal Questions:
At Home in the Body

- Think back to your years in high school or college. Who helped you learn how to function as a female? Name as many people as you can remember and identify what s/he awakened in you.

- Consider each subsequent time period, remembering many different kinds of teachers in your life and experiences that helped you understand your sexuality as a woman from the inside out.

Affirmations for Being Female

Something about Esther attracted Hegai and brought her special attention. In his own way Hegai was a mentor for Esther, because he helped to ground her cultural and spiritual identity in her woman's body. He blessed her identity as a female, as only such a connoisseur could.

We live in a culture without ritual separation from mother and father. Easy divorce and contraception mean that sexuality is no longer a substitute separation. We are no longer "owned" by a father and then a husband. Our independence means we must take full responsibility for our body-selves at a very early age, without the protective institutional structures that once shielded women, at least through their child-bearing years. In our quest for wholeness and integration of body, soul and form in the work world, we must come to terms with the power and promise that God created us for partnership with men and that means claiming our full potential as women.

I see now that I have made it very difficult for anyone to encourage the feminine side of me. I realize that I could not receive the affirmation for being female from my own husband until I had done the inner work of separating from my father. Therapy and sharing my own story with other women have helped me do some of that inner work.

There have also been several significant older men who sought me out among more beautiful women. Because they carried some part of my father's authority, they had the power to bless my undernourished feminine side and I am deeply grateful. I understand those relationships as part of God's call to discover the goodness of my own sexual identity.

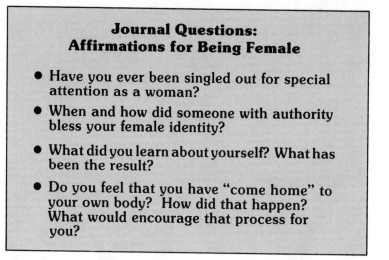

**Journal Questions:
Affirmations for Being Female**

- Have you ever been singled out for special attention as a woman?
- When and how did someone with authority bless your female identity?
- What did you learn about yourself? What has been the result?
- Do you feel that you have "come home" to your own body? How did that happen? What would encourage that process for you?

Conclusion

My own path to reclaiming my sexual identity began with choosing to say "No," as Vashti did, to the common view that my sexual self belonged to my husband rather than to me. As my own isolation from other women began to break down, I learned to speak of my own sexual feelings and to understand how language barriers had limited my ability to interpret and integrate my own body experience.

Take some time to reflect on any body experiences that have been "good news" for you. Then consider other relationships which were not consummated sexually, which aroused sexual feelings. Feel the aliveness those memories bring to your body. When we keep our sexual feelings deadened for fear they will ensnare us somehow, we lose the essence of our sexual power as women.

6. CHANGE OR DIE!

Mordecai's terrible dream of the two dragons fighting became reality when Haman, the king's chancellor, determined to kill all the Jews. Esther's cultural role as queen clashed with her own spiritual heritage in the dispute between Haman and Mordecai. Finally, the battle took place in her own body and soul, until she made a decision to act. This struggle was the turning point in bringing Esther's braided streams back together again. Her effort must be ours as well. We must move beyond cultural stereotypes and integrate our own braided streams or die in spirit.

Different Views of Reality

Haman was the king's chancellor, in charge of all matters of state. His responsibility was to secure the king's power over the vast domain. Haman had to deal with local grievances and use both military power and economic favors to keep a certain level of insecurity going, undercutting any local leaders who were getting too powerful. Haman had a good network of informers among the governors, and he watched for any signs of too much cooperation among them. Misplaced loyalty could spell trouble for the king.

Haman loved order, perfection and control. He had the power to eliminate opposition and to cripple competition. He hated his rivals, and he believed that life was simply a struggle for survival. Haman was ambitious: he enjoyed the power he had and stamped out opposition wherever he could.

After Haman was appointed chief advisor to the king, every man had to bow before Haman in recognition of his authority. Mordecai refused to bow. As a Jew, Mordecai bowed only before God. When this was reported to Haman, the king's chancellor was furious. Haman determined to kill all the Jews in revenge for Mordecai's disloyalty.

Many Jews in exile struggled with the issue of bowing before a foreign authority. The first commandment prohibited honoring other gods. Daniel had been imprisoned for his refusal to bow before Nebuchadnezzar, the Babylonian king; the Jewish prophets castigated Hebrews who honored foreign gods. For Mordecai then, refusal to bow to Haman was a statement of faith. As Haman realized, Mordecai was indeed claiming allegiance to a power beyond the political sphere which Haman could control. It was a clash of two cultures, two different belief systems, two views of life itself.

Haman believed life was "nasty, brutish and short" and that power meant control in the struggle for survival. Mordecai operated out of a covenant with God that gave hope for his people, even if his personal life had to be forfeited. Haman had no god but himself. Mordecai interpreted his life through the Exodus story, the promise of David's line, and prophetic teachings about God's judgment and ultimate love for Israel. Haman wanted uniformity and control; he knew he was right! Mordecai put his faith in God's powers, in the diversity of creation that would allow the Hebrews to survive in a hostile environment. Haman's view of reality was mechanical, hierarchical and rigid. Mordecai's view was larger, more mystical and more organic.

Haman's view of reality allowed for no diversity, no disagreement and *no newness!* There was no place for oddity. In his abstract hierarchical system, weakness and suffering had no meaning or purpose. Life was a constant battle.

Haman had an "either-or" view of reality: either he was in charge and Mordecai could be eliminated, or he wasn't. There is no evidence that Haman considered an alternative, in which he and Mordecai might hold different loyalties and still live together. As a Jew who had decided to stay in the Persian capital, Mordecai clearly did see that possibility.

Mordecai's view of reality, based on the Jews' covenant with the one God of all creation, gave him a way to oppose Haman's interpretation of reality. If, instead of a rigid power structure based on death, there was an organic sense of continuing creation going on through the history of the Jews, then all parts had purpose. Human life and death had meaning. Because Mordecai understood God's promise through a whole people over time, he could act with freedom in the face of Haman's threat of death. Mordecai was not afraid of the possibility that he would be killed for disobeying Haman's order.

But, then, Haman decided to kill all the Jews in the empire! That decision presented a different threat to Mordecai than personal death. Like Hitler's "final solution," Haman tried to assert his view of reality by eliminating his opposition. He wanted a "pure" political situation under his control. Haman precipitated a confrontation over which view of the universe was true!

Mordecai reacted to Haman's edict with a healthy fear. He tore his clothes and put on sackcloth, as a sign of mourning and humility before God. His response was bodily and direct. Because the Hebrews did not separate physical and spiritual matters, Mordecai's physical mortification was an outward sign of his inward anguish.

Mordecai entered the fray with Haman from a position of utter humility, utter powerlessness. Mordecai cried out to God for a miracle, to save the Hebrews from certain death. He acted out his prayer without words. He stood in judgment again Haman's perfectionism and purity, against Haman's pretense of control.

Like Haman, most of us talk from a hierarchical closed system, in which thought is organized in dualisms; up/down, right/wrong, either/or, light/dark, body/soul, male/female, etc. In the church this is prevalent as well. Our own speech is closer to Haman's value system than Mordecai's, at least in the public sphere. We behave as though the universe were governed by neutral physical laws that we, through our technology, can control. Have we not fallen victim to the very sin of pride that the story of Eden warns against: the sin of thinking we are in control? Haman's view of reality dominates American culture.

Beneath the public level of economic power and political control, do women also know Mordecai's reality? Recent feminist literature suggests that women do have a complex and frequently unconscious sense of connection with life beyond the quantifiable conception of reality that permeates our language. Women see beyond the surface. Women operate with Mordecai's spiritual belief system, although they are often immobilized from acting on that awareness by fear of ridicule for their "other knowing."

In my own life the struggle between Haman's reality and Mordecai's larger vision takes form around money and work. My cultural stereotype says that money is the measure of real worth in our society. Money provides control and choice for the "haves," and it limits options for the "have-nots." More important, it divides our society along the lines of having money. This division means I either have to make money myself or marry money and hang onto the man who provides it. Our consumer culture divorces money from human relationship and meaningful physical work, and advertisements imply that spiritual value can be supplied with the power of choice that money brings. Haman's view of reality dominates the world of money, which symbolizes power and worth, status and choices in our society.

However, Mordecai's view permeates my job search, and I want my work to be part of God's call to develop my full potential as a woman, as part of God's image in the world. As Peter and I have moved from place to place, I have either found work as a teacher or created income as a potter or retreat leader. I know that my desire to be paid for work that I do comes from my own desire for power and control, not from a survival need. The desire to be paid is part of my vocational stream of finding a form for my creative energies in the external world.

But, for me, down underneath the question of money is the question of security. The "Haman" in me says, "Nobody else cares about you, so you better provide for yourself." The threat of annihilation that Haman posed comes to me in questions of health. What will happen when my own health fails? Who will provide for me then? My self image is so tied to being a pioneer woman that I scare myself with fears of illness and aging. That fear is fed by media stories about nursing homes full of feeble old women who cannot provide for themselves.

Mordecai embodies another reality: a community that is ongoing and interconnected. Within the context of the Jewish community, Mordecai can face the threat of death and move through it to cry out for change, for release! Mordecai made his own body a statement of opposition to Haman's view of reality. His action calls us to God's presence in the midst of crisis.

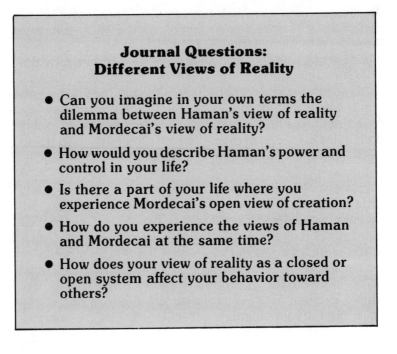

**Journal Questions:
Different Views of Reality**

- Can you imagine in your own terms the dilemma between Haman's view of reality and Mordecai's view of reality?

- How would you describe Haman's power and control in your life?

- Is there a part of your life where you experience Mordecai's open view of creation?

- How do you experience the views of Haman and Mordecai at the same time?

- How does your view of reality as a closed or open system affect your behavior toward others?

Change as Threat

Word came to Esther that Mordecai was sitting at the gate in sackcloth and ashes. From her background as a Jew, Esther knew that this was a sign of mourning, a sign of extreme penitence before God. But, her response was to deny Mordecai's sign. She sent a servant with a change of clothing for Mordecai, so he would not be imprisoned or sent away.

When Esther's servant brought Mordecai new clothing, he refused it and sent her a challenge: "Your people have been sold into death. Go to the king and plead for us!"

Esther refused, because she was afraid. "I will be killed if I go unbidden, and the king does not hold out his scepter. It's been more than a month since he has called for me; I dare not intrude."

Hiding behind her fear of change, her fear of challenging the king's rules, Esther refused to go. Even though she was the queen, she did not want to move out of her expected place. She could not see a fate for herself other than possible death. She was so used to being the silent figurehead, the dependent and supportive wife, that she was not in touch with her strength. She had over-identified with her female role and forgotten her spiritual stream.

Until this point in the story, Esther had known herself through the responses of other people. She had internalized the cultural messages of her living environment, symbolized by the king's story. She had not taken a stand against the demands of that culture, as Vashti did. She had learned her faith from Mordecai and, as a woman, had no place in the public worship life of her people. She had been schooled by Hegai in the most important skills she needed as a beauty in the court. She had been chosen queen and no doubt expected to live without significant change the rest of her life.

Esther was afraid to know why Mordecai was in sackcloth, because his mourning threatened the peace and security of her existence. She didn't want the change. She did not yet know the dilemma that Mordecai would reveal to her, but she could sense impending danger, and she reacted by trying to deal with the symptom.

We live in a society with the appearance of predictability; change is threatening. Technology promises mastery over the vagaries of nature and the arbitrariness of death. We live with the fantasy of permanence and close our eyes to the nearness of our mortal finitude as long as we can. We send the ill to hospitals and the old to nursing homes. We cordon the poor in decaying cities. As long as we can divorce ourselves from our body-knowing, we can continue to rape the planet of its resources and put our faith in money, the ultimate abstract god. We all participate in selective blindness, because it supports our standard of living. We deny the consequences as long as possible.

As women, we numb ourselves to keep the money system running smoothly; we want to fit in because we are comfortable. We apologize for success, and we try to avoid failure. Our interest in relationships is perverted by shutting out awareness with boredom or addictions. For the most part, we do not let ourselves know what we know. We do not allow our body-knowing to surface as thought, as choice, as action. Like Esther, we deny what we know with new clothes, or a busy schedule, or tranquilizers. We participate in the sin of Haman, wanting perfection instead of the untidy diversity of nature.

I, too, have denied the need for change, even when confronted directly. On my fortieth birthday, sixty people gathered at the church to celebrate that important passage. The people who gathered were a composite picture of my community. Peter and I had lived in one place for *three whole years,* and I felt rooted at Church of the Saviour. It was wonderful to celebrate so joyfully: job, home, friends, church, creative new work emerging...just what I wanted! I was living the fairy-tale ending after twenty years of moving and change.

Within a month after the celebration, Peter got orders to move to Germany, away from everything I valued except himself! My first reaction was to deny my part in it, to refuse to go at all. Then, I realized that I did not want to make the choice of refusal either. Like Esther, I tried to ignore the dilemma I would have to face.

The choice between Haman's system and Mordecai's challenge will come to all of us. No matter how safe and secure our lives are, Mordecai will appear at the gate in sackcloth and ashes, challenging us to risk death in favor of new and fuller life.

Or perhaps you will face Haman through widowhood or divorce. Or, if you have identified more strongly with your vocational stream and have achieved in "a man's world," the time may come when you decide to have children...with no success. Mordecai's challenge to you will be to find a way to experience mothering without bearing children.

However the upset comes, you may be assured that it will. Haman comes to us all. Like the demon in the desert who tempted Jesus before he began his ministry, Haman will threaten you with death. And Mordecai will come in a dream or a person to challenge you with a choice that must be made for life. That is the crisis of midlife, when a woman must face the terror of claiming her full self.

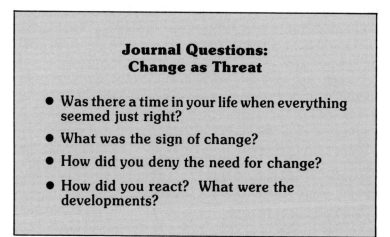

Journal Questions: Change as Threat

● Was there a time in your life when everything seemed just right?

● What was the sign of change?

● How did you deny the need for change?

● How did you react? What were the developments?

Time to Change

At first, Esther refused to go to the king because she was afraid for her life. Seeking an audience with the king would reveal her identity as a Jew, the very group Haman wanted to eliminate. For Esther, the risk was extreme: she could be killed if the king did not respond.

Facing his own threat of death from Haman, Mordecai issued a challenge to Esther which put her in a "no-win" situation: death was on either side. For Esther, it was a mixture of public and personal crisis. If she did *not* go into the king's chamber, she would die in a public slaughter. If she *did* go, she might lose her own life because she had broken the king's prerogative to choose, to control.

Then, Mordecai spoke the line that made the Book of Esther famous down through the ages: *"Who knows but that you were born for just such a time as this!"* (Es. 4:14, *RSV*). His verbal challenge was a call to meaning and purpose. Esther's response would be the turning point between living out her life as a reflection of what men saw in her or choosing her own life.

The question of timing is raised by Mordecai's challenge. How do we know when to act? Who can tell us when to speak and when to keep silence? Is it enough to play it safe and avoid going where we are not already wanted? How can we decide when to take a risk and confront the conventional norms?

Women are born to change and grow, to be reborn spiritually, sometimes at great risk and with much pain. Jesus surely showed us that much. Many of us choose a living death by denying the creative energies that continue long after we have produced a couple of children. Mental hospitals are full of women who turn their energies inward, and tranquilizers keep many others numb to pain that could split the shells that hold them dumbly.

Making choices to grow can be painful. My own dilemma about the choice of staying in the States was difficult and necessary for claiming my life as a woman. My shell had begun to crack open through the Women's Ministry of Faith at Work and through teaching at Church of the Saviour. If I moved away from those institutional structures, I would once again be at a beginner's point in finding a safe place to share my gifts. I was also afraid of feeling boxed-in by the Army expectations of our "coupleness," which would be heightened in a foreign county. I had not lived on an Army post for ten years, and I dreaded becoming "a dependent" again.

On the other side of my dilemma was the importance of my relationship with Peter. He is no Haman! In fact, he is a believer like Mordecai, with faith in the creative possibilities of change. I was afraid that choosing to stay would put our marriage in jeopardy, but choosing to go would put my soul in despair.

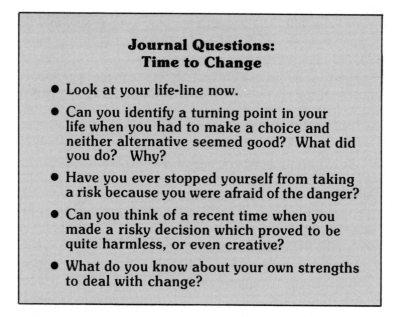

Journal Questions:
Time to Change

- Look at your life-line now.

- Can you identify a turning point in your life when you had to make a choice and neither alternative seemed good? What did you do? Why?

- Have you ever stopped yourself from taking a risk because you were afraid of the danger?

- Can you think of a recent time when you made a risky decision which proved to be quite harmless, or even creative?

- What do you know about your own strengths to deal with change?

Making a Choice

So, Esther told Mordecai, "I can't. Suppose he has me killed?"

Her cousin Mordecai replied by messenger, "Don't think you will escape because you are the Queen! If you refuse, then God will find another way to save us, but you will die!"

What a statement of faith! And what an awful challenge! The covenant would continue to operate, whether she obeyed his summons or not. Although Mordecai asked Esther to face the possibility of death, he also reminded her of the larger context in which she could make this decision. The context for her choice went beyond the Persian culture and the king's power over her body. With his terrible challenge, Mordecai called Esther to explore her own relationship to God.

Most of us do not find ourselves in the middle of a national crisis like Esther's. Instead, we hear the words of call as a personal challenge, a challenge to welcome the tributary streams of our lives into a deepening river of soul and self. Sometimes the call comes with pain and suffering. It always involves a choice.

How do we know when to act? How can we recognize the occasion for breakthrough among the different streams we have kept separated? We can think logically and rationally, identifying all the possible ramifications and even assigning numerical values to consider quality, as well as quantity.

We can also involve the right brain, through art and feeling and prayer, to comprehend more fully what is "at stake." In addition we can attend to our body pains, stress reactions and emotional life. At some point all the logic and learning, all the advice and advocacy, all the dreams and intuitions and agonized prayers give way to action and risk.

I was finally pushed to a choice: go with Peter or stay in the States. My own cultural expectations were clear: I would leave what I loved and move with my husband because his orders came from a higher authority. But during the winter of 1980, I helped to design and lead the first Women's Event for Faith at Work, and I felt my vocational stream running deeper and faster, urging me to stay.

At first I could only see the two alternatives: to go or to stay. As much as I felt I couldn't go, I also believed that I could not choose a two-year separation without destroying our marriage. I began to think about grouping my work assignments so I could come back to the States and still be with Peter in Germany part of the year. With my spiritual director I kept writing and praying and exploring ways to honor my own call to wholeness as a woman. This was a critical time in my own development. I also knew my decision would affect the patterns of our marriage, as Peter looked ahead toward retirement from the Army.

Other events fed into the ongoing decision process. During the summer of 1980, Peter's father died suddenly, and we helped his mother move from Washington, D.C. to Spokane, Washington. Then my father became seriously ill and had major surgery, which meant I did not want to leave the country immediately. Peter left that August, and I stayed to complete my retreat schedule and be with my parents, planning to join him at Thanksgiving.

My decision was made by a combination of inner and outer events. As I decided to stay behind, my body felt centered but not joyful. I knew it was right for me.

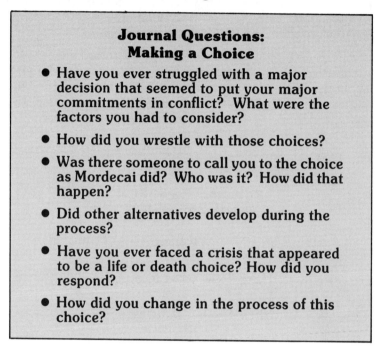

Journal Questions: Making a Choice

- Have you ever struggled with a major decision that seemed to put your major commitments in conflict? What were the factors you had to consider?

- How did you wrestle with those choices?

- Was there someone to call you to the choice as Mordecai did? Who was it? How did that happen?

- Did other alternatives develop during the process?

- Have you ever faced a crisis that appeared to be a life or death choice? How did you respond?

- How did you change in the process of this choice?

Facing Mortality

My personal sense of crisis deepened during the fall of 1980, quite apart from the decision not to accompany Peter to Germany. Friends from the church rented our house, furnished, so I cleared my pottery studio and stored personal belongings there. Then, I drove to Chicago and lived out of a suitcase and a friend's basement for three months. I felt like my whole world was collapsing, and I wondered if I was being punished for being a bad wife!

After all the confusion of the move and the change, I went to the doctor in October for a routine birthday physical. He found ovarian cysts on both sides, and after two days of tests, told me he suspected cancer. I sat in his office and cried. My body seemed like the last safe place left in my life and now even that was diseased! I needed to decide whether to have surgery, how to pay for it and where to go! Suddenly, I was faced with a life and death decision, like Esther's.

After a battery of hospital tests that supported the doctor's diagnosis, I decided to stay in Chicago and have the surgery. My body was ready to act even while my mind was resisting the choice! I still planned to get to Germany by Thanksgiving if I could do it!

Journal Questions:
Facing Mortality

- Have you ever faced the threat of physical death?
- How did you know what to do?

Conclusion

Haman symbolized the limits of a closed political system based on power and control. Such a closed system of thinking could not change without destruction. Mordecai believed that God was bigger and more creative than Haman's system. It was Mordecai, not Haman, who caused the crisis! Mordecai confronted Haman's view of reality with a different view that would embrace "unassimilated peoples."

Mordecai confronted Esther with the challenge that she was uniquely placed and should prepare to face the king on behalf of her people. Symbolically, Mordecai challenged Esther to let go of her dependence on men and their systems, to allow the streams of life to converge.

Finally Esther's choice was to change or to die!

7. STREAMS CONVERGING
God's Presence as a Body Experience

Esther sent a message by way of her servant to Mordecai: "Assemble the Jews of Susa and fast with me for three days, after which I will go to the King."

Why this time of preparation, if she had already decided to go?

Esther spent three days alone in the darkness of her soul, face-to-face with God. She took off her robes of office, gave up her nascent will, let go of the Jewish law, and stopped taking food to sustain her body. She died to her past securities, so she could live from her own body center. Esther's time of fasting and prayer stands as a counter-balance to Hegai's cultural preparation (see Chapter 5).

Esther moved from denial, down through fear and refusal, diving deep into her own soul for truth and courage. Unlike Vashti, Esther did not act with haste. Instead, she confronted the bodily consequences of her choice and then opened herself to whatever lay ahead.

Fasting

The traditional background for Esther's fast came from the annual day of atonement required by Mosaic law in which all Jews were to be in sorrow and affliction for their sins (Lev. 23:27). Other fasts were called in times of national emergency, as when Judah was invaded (2 Chron. 20:1-4). Generally, fasting meant abstaining from food but not water. The fast that Esther called was extreme, for she abstained from both!

The posture of Esther and her supporters outside the palace was one of confession, admitting their own inability to deal with the situation they faced. Their stance was a direct contrast to Haman's: he assumed that he was in total control of the situation.

Fasting signaled relinquishment of self-feeding on behalf of something more sustaining. Esther would have remembered the story of the manna provided the Jews during their Exodus wandering in the desert, as a sign of God's provision. We might also think of the reply which Jesus made during his own forty-day fast: "You shall not live by bread alone, but by every word that proceeds from the mouth of God" (Matt. 4:4).

Fasting is a tangible way of opening our lives to God. It awakens our senses to the spiritual dimension of matter. In our culture where food is used and abused as a substitute for companionship and intimacy, going without food can be an act of acknowledging the presence of God in all parts of creation: in both pain and pleasure, among the poor and the rich. Fasting awakens our bodies to spiritual connections and opens our lives to God.

Fasting is also a statement of faith, making prayer a whole-body act! Corporate fasting is a powerful way for women to acknowledge their spiritual quest together. Women are often stereotyped as being more grounded in bodily functions (earthy, sensual, dark and bloody), but we know how separated we can be from our bodies. Fasting can awaken our minds to the cosmic forces in our bodies. We can move beyond the surface images and awaken interconnections that we dull in ordinary patterns of life.

Fasting and prayer were the beginning of my preparation for facing surgery. After making arrangements to enter a local hospital in Chicago, I spent the preceding weekend at a Faith at Work Women's Event called "Turning Points in My Life as a Woman." I knew that event would be a good place to face whatever lay ahead. Since my father was a doctor, I had been suspicious of unnecessary female surgery all my life, and I considered my body "a trust" for which I was responsible. Still, I wanted to open my soul to whatever truth my body held.

I spent the weekend on a juice fast, letting my body cleanse itself of unnecessary toxins. As my mind cleared because of the fast, it was easy to enter into Biblical stories of women with Jesus and experience the reality of healing touch from those stories. On Sunday of the Women's Event, we had a meditation on Mary, the mother of Jesus. I allowed the words of scripture to enliven my inward images and filled my journal with drawings and dialogue, entering deeply into an experience of being held by Mary. When I signed into the hospital that Sunday evening, my body felt light, even transparent. A close friend stayed with me, helping me to relax with a guided meditation. I felt ready for death or life, and very close to Mary.

Have you ever had a dream or meditation image that seemed to wrap around your conscious mind, like a mood or a song? That was the sensation I had. My body was aware of being held within a spiritual presence of love and tender care. This experience felt like the dissolving of a barrier between body and spirit, the merging of the two realities.

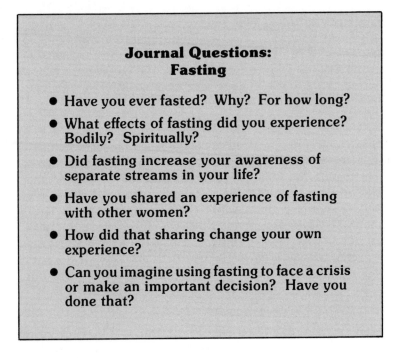

**Journal Questions:
Fasting**

- Have you ever fasted? Why? For how long?
- What effects of fasting did you experience?
  Bodily? Spiritually?
- Did fasting increase your awareness of
  separate streams in your life?
- Have you shared an experience of fasting
  with other women?
- How did that sharing change your own
  experience?
- Can you imagine using fasting to face a crisis
  or make an important decision? Have you
  done that?

Choosing Life

During her three days of fasting, Esther came face-to-face
with God in prayer (Es. 4:17, *JB*). "Remember, Lord," she
prayed, recalling the story of how God had delivered the
Israelites in earlier crises, "and reveal yourself in the time of
our distress."

She believed that God would not abandon her or her
people, but she clearly needed to spend the time intentionally opening her soul to God for the saving work to be done
through her.

"As for me," she continued, "give me courage." She did
not pray for success or even for safety. Her prayer was a
prayer for relationship, for timing, for unfolding awareness
as events developed. Esther was not picturing how God
would act in this affair, but was opening herself for whatever
would be required of her.

Esther's prayer was a statement of her spiritual development, an expression of her change from a willing and
obedient servant, learning the rules of the past, to a mature
and *self* conscious woman in charge of her own relationship
with God. In a philosophical sense Esther was now ready to
make ethical decisions because she knew herself. In a moral
sense she could now love more fully because she could
choose to give her own life to or for another.

In her prayer Esther cried out to God, "I am alone and...am
about to take my life in my hands." No one could protect her
anymore. She had moved beyond Mordecai and her
religious community. She stood without her robes of power,
without the comfort of food, without the promise of success.
It was a moment of unity and wholeness and terror! Esther
then ended her prayer with the plea, "...and free me from my
fear" (Es. 4:17z, *JB*).

Her plea was both a cry of anguish and a life choice. Up to
this point in the story, Esther derived her self-image from the
different men who reflected parts of her strength. The king
embodied a culture in which beauty gave her access to
power; Mordecai interpreted her faith community and
taught her skill in the political world of the Persian court;
Hegai encouraged her female sexual identity within the
dominant cultural norms; and Haman catalyzed her spiritual
calling with his callous determination to exterminate her
people. But finally, Esther stood alone with God, face-to-
face, claiming her own choice, taking her life into her own
hands!

Esther's ability to risk her life did *not* do away with her fear.
Instead, she embraced her fear and her courage. She knew
she was only human and could indeed be killed. She also
knew that she was part of a larger design, part of God's
continuing revelation of purpose for all of creation. And it
was *in her body* that Esther knew when to act. She knew that
physical death might be the result of her choice; she felt both
her fear and her strength. She was free, finally, to make her
decision.

The years Esther spent learning from Mordecai and Hegai,
and even from the king, were not wasted. Even the catalytic

evil of Haman had its purpose—to challenge Esther with the moment of ethical choice when she stood alone and aware of her own power and personhood. Esther was fully alive at the very moment when she was choosing to risk death!

Women who stand alone with God, facing death either in a literal or figurative sense, bring years of experience in separated streams to the moment of breakthrough into wholeness. They are not beginners, like Vashti! If they have done the work of developing each stream fully within the frame of their own lives, then they will emerge centered in their own bodies, ready to live life from the inside out. Resurrection begins.

Does the passage into spiritual maturity have to be marked by a life or death choice?

Personally, I believe that it does. At some point we have eyes to see and ears to hear the limits of the life we are now living. We understand that there is no ultimate safety, just as Esther did. Death lies at the end of choosing either risk or safety. But, if we choose risk, then we can open ourselves to God's purpose, to the courage to act when our culture invites us to stay deadened and asleep.

When each of us stands alone and aware that we, too, will die, no matter what choice we make, then we *can* choose to act on behalf of others who have no voice, who have no power, who do not know how to open themselves to God's creative energy.

Many women turn back at the point of choosing risk, afraid of the consequences, unable to trust the creative possibilities of darkness and death. They choose known existence over risk and resurrection.

When I made the choice to "take my life in my own hands"—remaining in the States, choosing surgery—I was choosing risk. But, with pain and embarrassment, I can now see that many other times in my life I turned away from choices that were not as drastic as the life-death choice. I have dulled my awareness with drink or food, or I have gotten sick as a way of avoiding what I needed to do.

I know that sickness can be a substitute for spiritual growth. I also know that the disease symptoms which brought me to surgery felt like guidance from God, because they helped me to let go of my body as an object. I did not praise or worship my body in the cultural sense, but I still carried a childhood fear that my body would "get me into trouble," and I alternately regarded my body as a workhorse and an adversary. Recognizing that my body was in trouble, and that I needed all of the streams of my being to stay conscious and connected in my body, made my choice to have surgery a profound and mystical experience!

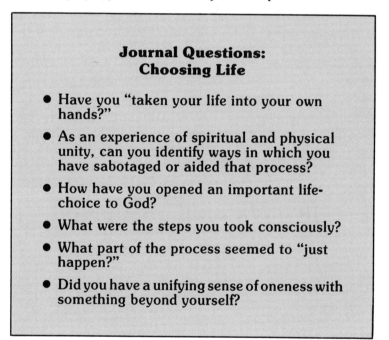

Journal Questions:
Choosing Life

- Have you "taken your life into your own hands?"

- As an experience of spiritual and physical unity, can you identify ways in which you have sabotaged or aided that process?

- How have you opened an important life-choice to God?

- What were the steps you took consciously?

- What part of the process seemed to "just happen?"

- Did you have a unifying sense of oneness with something beyond yourself?

Esther's Reality

After Esther passed through her personal confrontation with fear and recognized the streams of her own life merging, she was ready to act. From her solitary stance of utter humility in sackcloth and ashes, Esther moved to her strongest channel, her sexual role identity. To her female identity, she brought a stronger, clearer experience of God and a vision for how to proceed in confronting the king. Public action was the least developed stream of her life, since she had been content to stay in the cloistered chambers of the king's harem until Haman's threat came.

After her three days of fasting and praying, Esther was ready to act. She entered the royal chamber, dressed in her finest robes. "Rosy with the full flush of her beauty, her face radiated joy and love; but her heart shrank with fear" (Es. 5:1c, *JB*).

Were Esther's fears without cause? Or did prayer "open up" the situation? In fact, we cannot know. In story, the truth is clear: without God's presence, Esther would have been killed. Without her act of opening herself to God's guidance, she would have suffered Vashti's fate.

The different streams in Esther's life came together in this scene. She put on her royal robes, claiming the power of her office in the polity. She exerted all of her feminine charms. And she stayed centered in God's timing through her own body sense. At first the king was furious, but when Esther began to faint, his heart was changed: he held out his scepter and received her. Instead of punishing her by death, he offered her up to half of his kingdom. But instead of asking him for a portion of his power, Esther asked him to dinner!

After all of Esther's argument with Mordecai and the agony of her decision, asking the king to dinner seemed anticlimatic. But, the invitation fit the story symbolically, as well as dramatically. Esther stepped slowly and carefully into the terrible dilemma that still threatened her with death if her timing was wrong.

There was no one else to act for Esther. She had to act without guarantees, but she had the history of God's faithfulness to the Hebrews in times of distress and her own sense of God's incarnation through herself. These assurances empowered her spiritually. Esther engaged with God in a strategy that brought together all of her so-called masculine and feminine characteristics. She not only met the king on his own ground, but she also met her enemy, Haman. She invited the two men to her quarters.

Esther also drew her personal power from the other streams of her life: the sexual overtones of her private chambers in the palace and the motherly overtones of her skill with food. Her private quarters were like an extension of her body—enclosed, intimate and personal. When she invited Haman and the king into that space, she was relinquishing her only refuge. Esther was acting from a different "home" than her living space. She was able to open her personal quarters because she was centered in the cosmic presence of God, not in the particular place that was physically hers.

Esther's reality was different from Haman's rigid and cut-throat hierarchical system. Her power did not derive from the culture. She controlled no troops to exert a different kind of power. Even though she came from a Hebrew community whose people shared a strong religious heritage, she had not official role there. Esther's reality began with *her own body* and God's empowering spirit there. Her resources for influencing the king's decision were part of her own body— her beauty, her manner, her personal ties with the king.

Women operate from a different sense of reality than men do. Anne Wilson Schaef, in her important book *Women's Reality,* describes the White Male System, which could be Haman's or King Xerxes' system. It is uniform and exclusive, and therefore does not allow for the possibility of another reality system to operate at the same time. In a wonderfully intuitive way, Anne Schaef recognizes a different reality for women which, although not dependent upon religious convictions, includes a level of spiritual awareness.

I experienced this different reality during the time I was in the hospital. I finally recognized all the fears that had kept me bound to hard work and self-sufficiency. I was not able to care for myself at that time, and I had no assurance that my health would return. I had done everything I could think of to prepare myself for surgery: fasting opened my body to God's presence; sharing the retreat with other women opened my sense of community and family; and I felt protected by a mother when my friend Marianne interceded for me with the hospital staff. That night, before the surgery, Marianne and I shared an informal Eucharist, and then I fell asleep. (Sleeping seemed anti-climatic to me!)

During the night, I had a dream that was humorous and reassuring. In the dream I was startled by a piercing scream coming from a basement window. When I entered the basement, it was full of office equipment and people who were ignoring the scream coming from behind a brick wall. As I tore down the wall with my own hands, I could see a dinosaur trapped inside.

The next morning before going into surgery, I drew the dream. I realized that the dinosaur looked like a womb and ovaries! Having released the trapped animal in my dream, I was ready to let go of that trapped part of my own body.

The reality of how the streams in my life had been separated became clear after my surgery, as I grieved for the children I never had *and* awakened to new joy in my sexual identity. I went from the hospital to Germany, where Peter was then stationed. For the next few months, the isolation of being without my community of friends gave me the time to receive the care and protection from him that I had never been able to take in before. And I had plenty of time to live into my feelings of grief, loss and helplessness, without any work commitments to short-circuit that process.

While some women need to learn how to "stand up and walk alone," I needed to learn how to rest and receive love that had been there for me all along. Because I had identified so thoroughly with my vocational and spiritual streams, I had not embraced the dependent aspect of myself. Now that the possibility of being locked into the mothering role for twenty years (my scary image of being a mother) was gone, I could explore the mother in me more freely. This freedom has brought a degree of tenderness and mercy to my closest relationships that I did not know was possible. I felt the streams of my life beginning to touch, if not merge.

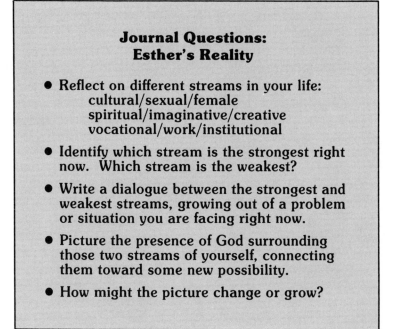

**Journal Questions:
Esther's Reality**

● Reflect on different streams in your life:
cultural/sexual/female
spiritual/imaginative/creative
vocational/work/institutional

● Identify which stream is the strongest right
now. Which stream is the weakest?

● Write a dialogue between the strongest and
weakest streams, growing out of a problem
or situation you are facing right now.

● Picture the presence of God surrounding
those two streams of yourself, connecting
them toward some new possibility.

● How might the picture change or grow?

Conclusion

The streams of Esther's life converged in her body as she
entered the king's chamber. Finally, she knew how to use all
the parts of her life together. Our own life streams develop
separately, in response to different authority figures *outside*
of our lives. Then, at some critical point, we experience a
different level of reality that is open-ended and not familiar.
The source of authority has shifted from outside to inside.
Then, the presence of God as a living part of our operating
system allows each of us to "take our lives in our own hands,"
as Esther did.

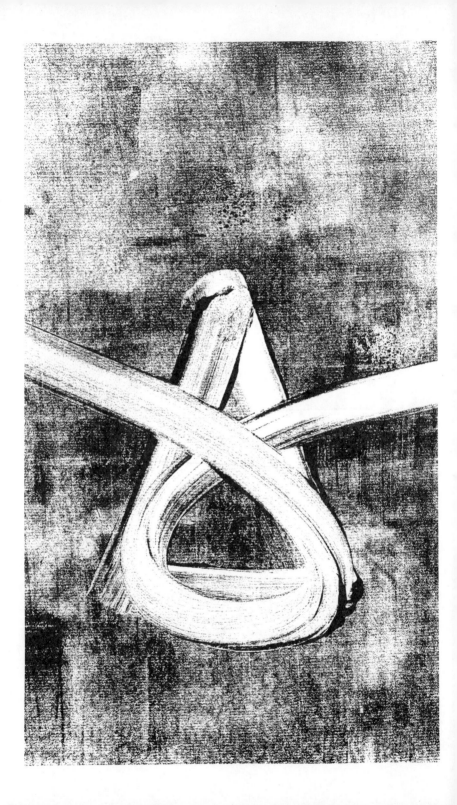

8. THE DINNER PARTY
Facing the Enemy

Esther experienced the reality of God in her own body as she went in to the king. This was the beginning of convergence for Esther. She expanded God's empowering presence to the dinner party she gave for Haman and the king as the second stage of living "from the inside out."

The "Dinner Party" was Esther's way of living out her heritage from Mordecai. Her own version of God's covenant with the Jews developed as she waited for her own sense of right timing for the request she still had to make.

Inviting the Enemy

Once Esther broke through the barrier of her own fear and the barrier of the king's rule to keep people away except by his request, she began to claim her authority in a wider arena: the two most powerful men in the kingdom!

Esther asked the king to come for a banquet in her private quarters and to bring Haman with him. Like a fulcrum, her invitation interrupted the flow of Haman's power which had been directed against the Jews with the full support of the king. She set the change in motion by making a simple social request. The king responded by ordering Haman to come: "Tell Haman to come at once, so that Esther may have her wish" (Es. 5:5, *RSV*).

Asking Haman extended Esther's personal decision to act into the battle between two different views of right, of power, of control. Her invitation signaled the beginning of a cosmic struggle around the table, although neither Haman nor the king was aware of that dimension at first. Haman interpreted Esther's invitation through his own belief system: he was flattered to be included. Later he bragged to family and friends about the honor of Esther's invitation.

Esther did not claim more authority than she had. In fact, she kept the real issue hidden until she had a sense that the timing was right. But, her silence did not mean she was stagnant. Like a tiny stream of water, finding its was down a flat plane, she moved slowly, letting each stage fill with her presence until the next step was clear.

If we want to change our cultural system, which denies the ways in which women grow and develop fully, then we must proceed as Esther did—slowly and carefully, from our own bodies as our spiritual center. We must invite our enemies to dine with us, simply and clearly. We must offer what we have, after doing the integrating work that Esther did.

We live in a hurrying culture, where efficiency and control pervade both language and work. Women know there is also another way to live, epitomized by the very young and the very old, in which clock time is suspended for fascination or remembering. When we bring the intuitive and feeling side of our knowing into play, then timing can become an act of attentiveness, of love. Without intuition and feeling, timing becomes just one more method of controlling others.

Do we seek the enemy face-to-face? Or do we seek the protection of personal guardians who are bigger, stronger or more experienced in dealing with brute control. As long as we avoid confronting the shadowy fears that keep us deadened to our own powers, we will not move into full maturity. If we choose the safety of marriage, so that a husband will buffer those encounters with evil, we will not know our own strength.

The enemy that I needed to invite to my own table was my prejudice against women. All the years that I had identified myself with work in the world made it difficult for me to identify with women who loved being at home with their children. The positive link came through my secondary stream, the spiritual-creative call to ministry that I had buried during my teenage years. My vocational stream, my mothering stream, and my spiritual stream came together in the Women's Ministry of Faith at Work.

Two members of the Women's Ministry Board had carried a dream during the seventies for Faith at Work to create some kind of learning event for women only. They wanted something that would honor mind and body, feelings and thinking, reflective silence and active ministry. One Board member had attended a gathering of Biblical feminists and seen a leader shouting angrily with her fist clenched in a macho power salute. Another member had read a book recommending that church women could revitalize boring marriages by greeting their husbands wrapped in saran wrap. "Surely there has to be something better for us!" they both said as we gathered to design the first event for women in the fall of 1979, months before my personal questions about my health and the move to Germany would surface.

As I worked on that design, I became interested. I had never attended a weekend for women only. I questioned the need for women to meet separately, to share stories of spiritual pilgrimages, but I noticed that the design process itself was more energizing than others with which I had been involved. We worked with Psalm 139 and I began to feel the womb-words in that marvelous praise of God's body-knowing:

> For thou didst form my inward parts,
> thou didst knit me together in my mother's womb...
> My frame was not hidden from thee,
> when I was being made in secret,
> intricately wrought in the depths of the earth.
> (Psalm 139:13)

I was meeting my own shadow at the table, waiting for the moment to request life and wholeness!

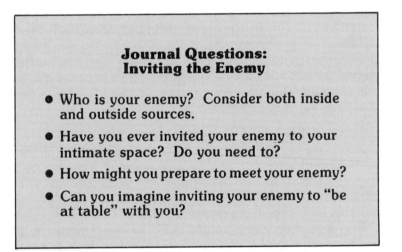

Journal Questions:
Inviting the Enemy

- Who is your enemy? Consider both inside and outside sources.

- Have you ever invited your enemy to your intimate space? Do you need to?

- How might you prepare to meet your enemy?

- Can you imagine inviting your enemy to "be at table" with you?

The Role of Food

Offering food to Haman and the king was such a homely act, such a feminine thing to do. When facing male power figures, we often try to use the same tactics that they do, but we come to such a confrontation with a physical disadvantage in size. Esther provides us with a different model.

By preparing a meal and serving it herself, Esther reclaimed a larger sense of her own womanhood than being just a beautiful face. She honored her public power as queen and her private favor with the king. She brought both her beauty and her nurturing qualities to the task at hand. She used the access that she had and depended upon her body sense of timing for the next step.

Sharing a meal with Haman and the king after her three-day fast recalled the importance of food and table fellowship among the Jews. If fasting was a sign of opening her life to God's possibility for new life, then sharing food was a sign of God's presence through her.

The food became a ceremonial way to reconcile parts of herself, as well as a strategy for confronting Haman and the king. Also, if she had let go of Jewish dietary laws when she entered the court, her preparation of the food might have symbolized reclaiming part of her spiritual heritage. Perhaps she was also reclaiming the mothering part of her own woman-self from a childhood that was starved for a mother's nurturing.

Esther was waiting, her body poised, for the right moment to make her request. She continued to be in the attitude of readiness, in the attitude of prayer, as she served the meal. When the king was primed and expecting her request, she simply asked them to return the next night. Esther's ability to wait until she sensed that the time was right revealed her God-centeredness.

No doubt Esther's three-day fast within the circle of prayer and fasting outside the palace included some kind of envisioning different outcomes and speculating different courses of action. In the end, she simply waited.

I am the Queen and I am a Jew,
  serving and waiting
    to speak
And you?

I am the King, full of good food
  ready to give
    what I have
up to half
  (for more would unbalance
    the scale.)

I'm Haman the guest
  drinking wine
    glad to release
what ties me in knots—
  that damn Jew
    who won't rise when I come
I'll forget him tonight
  and take in
    my reward
      my right
        my delight.

As modern American women, we often live like Haman, taking food and table company as a reward instead of a gift of relationship with the earth. We forget how powerful mealtimes can be. The spiritual quality of sharing food touches the most primal forces in every living creature, soothing the fear that there is not enough food to survive and sharing simple sustenance for life itself. The woman who knows the power of sharing food can invite people together in their humanness.

We live in a time when our culture seems to have forgotten the basic respect for land and water and seasonal food. We have become so caught up in technological control over the earth that we have destroyed parts of the food cycle without a second thought. Women, too, have lost their reverence for the land, for food, and for their part in sustaining life-drives among children. Instead, we have become a nation of people in a hurry, too busy for the simple ritual of eating together in reverence for aliveness, for God.

Sharing food symbolically is important for me. When we meet for classes at the School of Christian Living, our dinners together pave the way for sharing. When we meet on retreats, food preparation and clean-up are part of the design for developing community. Ritual meals are also an important way to end community when someone is moving away.

As I have faced critical times in my life, my own communion with Christ through the bread and wine of the Eucharist has also been essential. When I remember the bread and wine that I shared with my friend Marianne just before my surgery, I am reminded how very important these elements were to the sense of peace I felt. Somehow the words of institution and the actual ingestion of food helped to expand my awareness beyond the present crisis, so that I could glimpse the larger hope of resurrection, even as I was facing symbolic crucifixion.

Simply meditating on the connections behind what I am eating has become an act of reverence for the earth and the gift of life itself: the store where I bought the food and the people there; truck-drivers and farmers, seasonal laborers and local workers; conservationists and bankers; animal herds and plants adding their nutrients to the soil; eons of weather and erosion . . . Meditating on food also makes me aware of people in my own neighborhood who do not have enough food, or who do not know how to choose food that will keep them healthy on a limited budget.

What does it mean to share food with my enemy? Recently, I had the opportunity to sponge the naked body of a neighbor-lady who had fallen and broken several ribs. As I touched her aging flesh and smelled her skin odors, my own irritation (and shadow fears of being old or disabled and alone myself) drained away. I was truly sharing bread with her.

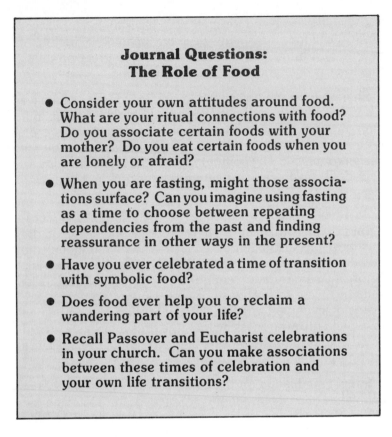

Journal Questions:
The Role of Food

- Consider your own attitudes around food. What are your ritual connections with food? Do you associate certain foods with your mother? Do you eat certain foods when you are lonely or afraid?

- When you are fasting, might those associations surface? Can you imagine using fasting as a time to choose between repeating dependencies from the past and finding reassurance in other ways in the present?

- Have you ever celebrated a time of transition with symbolic food?

- Does food ever help you to reclaim a wandering part of your life?

- Recall Passover and Eucharist celebrations in your church. Can you make associations between these times of celebration and your own life transitions?

Haman's Discomfort

Haman was proud to be included at the queen's table, and he did not sense that his power in the kingdom was being challenged. But, at the end of that first meal, Haman went home still troubled. "All of this does me no good as long as I see Mordecai the Jew sitting at the king's gate," Haman said (Es. 5:14, *RSV*).

Haman hated Mordecai because he did not acknowledge Haman's supreme authority. No amount of honor could fill

Haman's need for acclaim until everyone below him in the hierarchy acknowledged his position by bowing down. He believed that Mordecai's refusal to bow to him was just cause for Mordecai's death. When Haman complained to his wife and friends about Mordecai, they recommended that Haman not wait for the slaughter of Jews, but that he have a gallows built "and in the morning tell the king to have Mordecai hanged upon it; then go merrily with the king to the dinner" (Es 5:15, *RSV*).

Hanging as a source of merriment was one product of Haman's dehumanized value system. Haman could not allow Mordecai to demonstrate with his body posture that Haman was not in total control. Many of us picture God as being similar to Haman: an autocratic king or the supreme judge waiting to punish us for being independent. For many women the patriarchal church has reinforced that autocratic image of God as judge.

But the God of Esther was much more open-minded and present as a creator than a judge. Indeed, the image of God working through Esther to deliver the Jews is *active* in the world, not removed. God is on the side of diversity and independence. Esther's God was a companion and a guide, more than a judge who would keep women subordinate. God is on the side of change in this story.

My own experience of God in the past five years has been filled with wonder, as I meet with women on weekend retreats. The aspect of God that strikes me most when women meet without men is a different sense of time and space. We move in natural rhythms, sensing with our bodies when to work and play and worship. We care about the color and textures in a room, aware that making space for God means being creative with the space for ourselves, too. I've also noticed the respect we have for our differences and the desire we have to find a place for each person to contribute their part of God's unfolding truth. Welcoming our differences is the opposite of Haman's quest for total control!

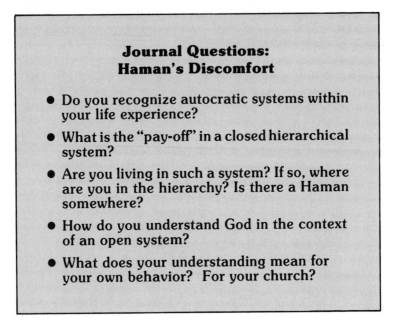

Journal Questions: Haman's Discomfort

- Do you recognize autocratic systems within your life experience?

- What is the "pay-off" in a closed hierarchical system?

- Are you living in such a system? If so, where are you in the hierarchy? Is there a Haman somewhere?

- How do you understand God in the context of an open system?

- What does your understanding mean for your own behavior? For your church?

The King's Discomfort

After the king left his dinner with Esther, he could not sleep. On the surface the evening had been perfect. But, we might say at an unconscious level, the king was aware of the tensions. His body was absorbing stress, though his mind could not name it.

The king had insomnia. In order to get back to sleep, he called for someone to read him the book of memorable deeds of the kingdom. When he heard an account of Mordecai uncovering a plot against the king's life, he asked if Mordecai had been rewarded. When he learned that no reward had been given, he determined to do something. He did not ask for guidance from God, but that did not limit God's creativity! Insomnia and midnight reading had a part in Esther's overall task, even though it was not directly related to her self understanding.

The king asked Haman how honor might be given to someone the king wanted to celebrate, and Haman, blind to other possibilities, described what he wanted for himself. When the recipient was named, Haman had to honor Mordecai by parading the Jew around the streets in the king's robes.

Haman kept encountering signs that his understanding of reality was too small, too narrow, and too closed. Parading Mordecai around the streets of Susa, shouting out the news of the king's favor, was an opportunity for Haman to see the failure ahead. Zeresh, his wife, could see that the tide of Haman's power had shifted. But Haman was so tied to his own perception of reality, that he risked death rather than change.

We can see that God was working through and beyond Esther. But there is a difference between a naive faith in God as a rescuer and a mature faith based on mutual action. In some way God needed Esther to bring other events toward convergence.

If Esther had stayed within the cultural expectations, the streams of her own life would have remained separated. There would be no story of deliverance for herself or the Jews. There would be no story of God made manifest through a woman who dared confront expected roles and behaviors.

If Esther had continued to deny the danger represented by Haman and held onto her myth of safety in marriage, God's creation would have been stifled or stilled. Do we hang onto old forms in the name of obedience?

The question for me is this: how do I know when breaking convention is God's will? The quick answer is, I don't! But the real answer is that I worry and pray and check my leadings with my spiritual mentors until I am ready to make a choice that seems life-giving.

When the question of whether I need to act against old patterns keeps me awake, I ask God for help. I suspect that wakefulness is a sign of guidance in the first place. If I am worried about something enough to have it wake me, then I know something in my body is trying to reach my consciousness. My own nature is deeply conservative, oriented to safety and control: I am a child of our culture. Change does not come naturally or easily, so the possibility of change is the first step in welcoming God.

I know, too, from the God of stories like Esther's, as well as from the life of Jesus, that God has a bias toward the poor, the oppressed and the outcasts. If I am wakeful because I sense a call away from cozy comfort toward stretching my life in new directions of compassion and justice, then I pay attention and watch for signs of God's presence. A sleepless night may well be God's call.

In the past I have spent time worrying about how to get back to sleep, instead of assuming that my body is one way for God to get my attention. Now when I can't sleep, I get up, open my journal and wait for God to speak. If I am worrying about a large decision, then I watch for particular daily steps to take.

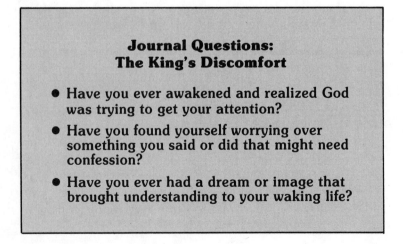

Journal Questions:
The King's Discomfort

- Have you ever awakened and realized God was trying to get your attention?

- Have you found yourself worrying over something you said or did that might need confession?

- Have you ever had a dream or image that brought understanding to your waking life?

God's Timing

Miraculous intervention played a part in Esther's story. Even though the king and Haman were not conscious of an extra-physical presence, God was surely acting through them as well as through Esther during this crucial period. Often we do not see a larger pattern in events that seem negative or difficult, until we look back from a certain time or distance. I have learned to be open for the miraculous intervention that goes beyond any plan. Like the king's dream, it signals the presence of God beyond my power to plan or protect myself.

One chilly winter night not long ago, I dropped Peter off at the church for his first silent retreat and drove back home. I parked the car and walked to the grocery store; I only needed a few items and the store was just six blocks away.

As I walked home, I had a fleeting sense of something wrong just before I heard quick running steps and then felt strong arms grab me as other hands pulled on my shoulder bag.

I clutched my groceries tightly against my purse and screamed aloud as I felt a fist punch my eye. Reeling, I kept yelling, hoping that somebody would open a door, and the boys would run away. I could see it was two black teenagers; they said nothing as we struggled in the dark.

One boy held me while the other kept hitting me until I fell. When they started kicking, I let go of my purse and they sped away. "Take the money and drop the purse!" I called after them, thinking of my ten-year-old leather bag I had carried so long. And then it was strangely quiet. Only my own sounds were left, as I picked up my groceries and tasted the cut in my mouth.

My first thought was to call a man, somebody strong, who would stay with me. I thought about Peter on his silent retreat about an hour's drive away. My car keys were now missing and besides, I was feeling too shaky to drive out there.

Then, below the inner voices, I realized there was a kind of stillness. A place of not-fear. I could not name what it was, but I drew closer to the stillness and decided to follow it if I could. Instead of calling anybody, I went downstairs to my pottery studio and trimmed pots for nearly an hour.

That routine activity has always been a prayer posture for me: turning a bowl upside down on the wheel, trimming away the excess clay with a tool, watching the thin curl of clay drop away from the foot-rim. That night it was a prayer of letting-go with my hands instead of words.

The next day when Peter returned, he was shocked! And then he was upset that I had not called someone. We both struggled with our feelings. He felt like a failure as husband and protector. I felt like I couldn't respond to his feelings at all. We both felt violated, unprotected, abandoned by God.

Three days afterward I wanted to go to my pottery studio downtown, because it would get me out of the house and give me a chance to talk about the incident instead of bottling it up inside. One eye was open, the other still puffy and bruised. I felt ugly and wounded, beaten and robbed of my safety as well as my money.

As I stood at the bus-stop, other people stared at me. I felt the pain some people have to live with every day if handicapped or disfigured. Again, I felt the stillness and a sense of learning for me in this experience.

The city bus pulled up, and I realized with a shock that the bus driver was black and there were no other passengers on the bus. Suddenly nausea swept over me, and I stood dumbly on the curb as the doors opened.

He looked at me and I just stood there.

"What beautiful hair you have!" he said, and my mouth dropped!

"Is it your own?" he asked. I nodded, stepping up into the bus.

"I mean, is it natural?" Again I nodded, forming words.

"I mean, it isn't a perm or anything?"

"No, it's always been like this," I said, touching my own short curly hair as though to make sure it was still mine.

"And what happened to your face?" he asked kindly, as I put money in the box and sat down across from him. So I told him.

We drove on while we talked, picking up other passengers. He scolded me for walking in our neighborhood after dark and told me about getting a citation for hitting an attacker like mine. He told me about his time in the Army as a sergeant and about his grandchildren.

And then we got to the end of the line, where we had to wait a few minutes before heading farther along his route. He looked at me and said quietly, "May I ask you a favor?"

"Sure," I said gratefully, glad for the way he had eased my embarrassment and fear.

"May I touch your hair?"

"Of course." So I leaned forward, and he touched it lightly.

Then he touched his own and said softly, "You know, it feels the same."

I sat transfixed, feeling the fear drain away from my body. "Be not afraid," his touch said, and I knew that I could walk on my street again, and shop at the grocery store, and not bar my heart against strangers. The bus driver had indeed provided a way through my fear. He was an instrument of miraculous intervention.

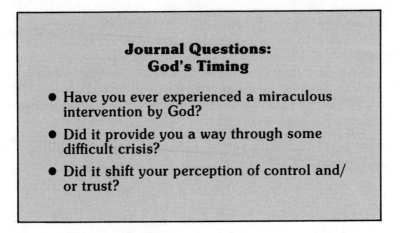

**Journal Questions:
God's Timing**

- Have you ever experienced a miraculous intervention by God?
- Did it provide you a way through some difficult crisis?
- Did it shift your perception of control and/or trust?

Conclusion

Esther's dinner party was the first step of Esther's journey outward from her body-centered spirituality. Confronting her enemy in the realm of her intimate and personal space meant that she could then walk freely into larger circles of conflict, because she was centered in her own body. Confronting the king at her table meant that she could transcend the cultural stereotype that kept women silent and "in their place" below men in the hierarchy. Esther met these two powerful men, not as an equal in their own system, but as a partner in God's system.

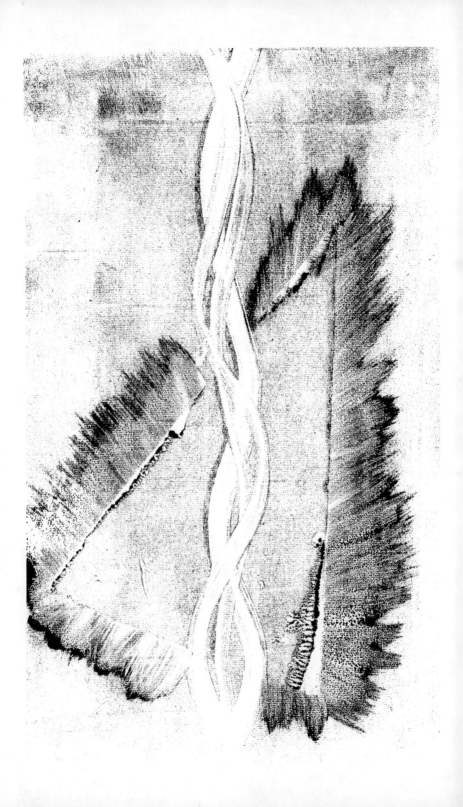

9. BREAKTHROUGH

Esther as an Advocate

Esther chose to press the king for the larger goal of safety for the Jews. In contrast to Vashti's choice for personal freedom, Esther wanted more than her own life. She wanted to speak for her people as well.

By continuing to extend her power in the court on behalf of her people, Esther named herself before the king. She chose to act even though she did not have permission from the legal system. And she stayed with the issue of changing the power structure within the kingdom, even when the king tried to keep his favor to her at the level of their personal relationship.

Extending Power

Esther served Haman and the king a second banquet. As they drank their wine, the king asked Esther again what she wanted. Again he offered her up to half the kingdom. Repetition of the scene heightened the drama and conveyed a sense of waiting for God's signal. Esther seemed centered, no longer fearful or hesitant. She was ready to speak when her time came.

When she sensed that the time was right, Esther framed her request to invite the king's positive response: "I ask for my life, and that of my people."

That single statement linked Esther with a vision larger than the view of saving her own life. In a sense she had already saved her life by confronting her own fears about being killed. She had already freed herself from the threat that had previously kept her from entering public life. Esther had already claimed her own life in relationship to God by risking it to enter the king's chambers.

Although Esther had passed through her personal fear, she spoke of her own life first, naming the value of her life to the king. She knew that the king could only relate to her people through her, because he had not changed his political viewpoint. He still saw himself at the top of a pyramid, in total control of the lives of people beneath him. He related to Esther in a personal way, and he had no intention of changing the structure of the kingdom to encourage diversity or make life easier for the Jews. He could grant personal favors and still retain full control for himself.

But Esther had changed. The hesitant girl was gone. If Haman catalyzed Esther's sense of herself, and the dinner party revealed her personal spiritual power, then her actual request unveiled her community connection. She did not directly challenge the king's power or source of authority, but she did not act as she was supposed to act under the old hierarchical system.

"If we had only been sold as slaves, I would not have asked," she said, "but we are faced with total annihilation!" Whether or not that was true, her statement suggested that the Jews could tolerate slavery within the range of their covenant faith. In fact, slavery was the key to Esther's own relationship with the king. Although Esther was the queen, she was also the king's slave: she had no legal rights before him. Everything she did in the public realm depended upon his personal favor.

Whether the king was aware of it or not, Esther was moving out of slavery into freedom through her own choice. Her willingness to risk death or defeat in confronting the king meant that she had changed the very basis of their relationship by her request. Esther was not begging for her life. She was bargaining as a woman, as a human being who could choose to risk her life.

Esther understood the king's value system, so she added an economic factor to her plea: "The persecutor cannot replace us as assets to the kingdom" (Es. 7:4, *RSV*). Her words linked private and public matters. Instead of the small cost of granting Esther a personal favor, the king now had to calculate the economic loss to his kingdom, as well as the loss of Esther, if he chose to refuse her request for mercy. She had linked their personal relationship with matters of state, while the king tried to keep them apart in order to retain control of the situation.

When Esther revealed that her people were to be killed, the king responded at a personal level: "Who is he and where is he that would presume to do this thing?" (Es. 7:5, *RSV*).

"Haman is the one!" Esther replied.

In a rage the king left the room. His choice was painfully clear. To side with Haman would mean losing Esther. To honor Esther's request would mean losing face in public, for the king could not reverse his own edict! There was no longer any way for him to keep public and private affairs separate.

Separation of public and private affairs keeps women confined in our society, too. Men control the institutional structures of our culture and women are in charge of raising children. This division is the cultural pattern with which we have grown up. Men with a hierarchical value system control the major money sources and parlay wealth through capital manipulation. Women generally hold peripheral and lower-paying jobs in the public sector, and they trade time and services instead of capital. As long as the public sector requires large amounts of money, and women are systematically denied access to institutional money structures, the money system will continue to exploit women and keep women from genuine partnership in public life.

We might consider a question similar to the one Esther raised about the economic value of the Jewish population: suppose our society were faced with the absence of women? How would our economy be affected? Are there ways to confront the systematic separation of public and private life in order to open ways for women to take a more active public role?

Although the patterns of our culture have opened somewhat, and some women have moved into the institutional structures of our public life, we have not seen a major shift in the internal structure of money, time and the definition of work. Somebody still has to care for the children! If women continue to be the primary care-takers for their own children (and that could change), then talented women will be entering the job market at midlife. How then can we restructure the work economy to admit the energy and creativity of women as their life-streams converge?

My own life may not be typical, but it is a common story. For twenty years I moved from place to place with my husband because I never questioned the assumption that his career was more important than mine. We both valued my contribution to our personal life together, but I did not commit myself to any institutional structure outside our home, except the church.

I see now that the cause for my lack of public involvement was not Peter's career, but my own family background. My father is a rugged individualist, and I grew up absorbing his anti-institutional prejudice. As long as I was living with the streams of my life running separately, I could not name the value of my life as a woman before the "cultural kings" at my own table. I could not choose life for myself or my people through an institutional structure. Thus, naming myself as part of a people was my first step in identifying the value of my own vocation.

My second step was to clarify my attitudes about money. I have always worked for money because pay made me feel competent. It was a way to retain a sense of my being and value in the external world as we moved away from different communities. In a way earning money substituted for the power of my father to name me as a real person. But, because I was female, I discounted the kind of work that I might consider doing. I never put any priority on my work over Peter's military career until the crisis of his orders to Germany. Then, I realized it was not the money but *doing* the work that really mattered to me. I could have found another way to earn money in Germany, but at the time I wanted to stay with the community of women associated with the Women's Ministry of Faith at Work.

The third step Peter and I had to take was to question the structure of our marriage relationship. If I was no longer willing to move every year or two, what could we do to accommodate my need? At a deeper level, what kind of time did we want to spend together and apart in the next phase of our life together? Could we find ways to keep our marriage firm enough to be valuable and loose enough to be growth-enhancing? As a start, we simply agreed that the two years Peter was in Germany would be turbulent and that neither of us would "bail out" in the midst of that chaos.

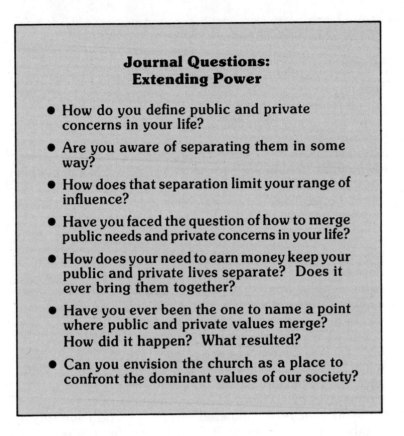

Journal Questions:
Extending Power

- How do you define public and private concerns in your life?

- Are you aware of separating them in some way?

- How does that separation limit your range of influence?

- Have you faced the question of how to merge public needs and private concerns in your life?

- How does your need to earn money keep your public and private lives separate? Does it ever bring them together?

- Have you ever been the one to name a point where public and private values merge? How did it happen? What resulted?

- Can you envision the church as a place to confront the dominant values of our society?

Staying Focused

After the king left the room where Esther finally made her request for mercy, Haman threw himself on Esther's couch to plead for his life. When the tide turned against him, Haman begged for the mercy which he had been unwilling to give the Jews.

When the king returned, he saw Haman lying on the queen's couch, and he assumed that Haman was trying to rape the queen! The king still saw Esther as his sexual property. The most important part of the offense to him was that he was a *witness* to what Haman was doing: "Is he going to rape the queen before my very eyes?" (Es. 8:8, *JB*). To the king it appeared that Haman was attacking the king's personal sphere of influence by attacking the queen.

Although Esther no longer was bound by the belief that she belonged to the king, she did not correct the king's perception. Because they were in her private quarters, anything that Haman did was encircled by Esther's most intimate presence. By inviting Haman and the king to be there in the first place, Esther made sure that the confrontation happened "on her turf," so to speak. Her careful strategy for confronting the king and Haman had also strengthened her trust in God's timing. Esther knew that she and her people ultimately belonged to God.

Esther did not "fall for" Haman, whether he was making a sexual advance or a plea for his life. She stayed focused on the larger issue of saving her people. Nevertheless, she did not press her question which had precipitated the confrontation at this time. The king was ready to fix his attention on Haman for trying to rape the queen. Esther wisely chose to let the king's own feelings eliminate Haman before she again raised the question of helping her people.

The king had Haman hanged on his own gallows and gave Haman's office to Mordecai. As far as the king was concerned, the matter was ended. Esther allowed her question to rest, but she did not forget the threat that the king's edict still posed for her people.

As modern American women living with the sexual freedom provided by contraception, we often "fall for" a sexual invitation, instead of undertaking the harder issue of changing the traditional patterns of a static marriage relationship or challenging the institutional structures of church, community or the work place. Like the king, our culture interprets most spiritual questions through the language and perceptions of sex. At midlife, when the streams of gender, vocation and spirituality dissolve the barriers of earlier separation and join into a single stream, we feel more alive, more coherent and more powerful than before. We become more attractive to certain men and may move into a love affair. Women, without the supportive structures to understand their sexuality in a broader spiritual and vocational context, may settle for an affair instead of wholeness.

We may also choose to withhold our sexual responsiveness from an ongoing relationship as a way to establish a sense of autonomy and choice. If we can understand that choice within the larger issue of personal integration, a marriage need not flounder over the issue of gaining sexual autonomy. Everything in our culture, however, pushes a woman toward responding when a man initiates a sexual invitation as the prerogative of marriage or male control. Either way, sexual expression can divert women from the larger issue of claiming the power of converging streams, from naming themselves.

My decision to travel between Germany and the United States between 1980 and 1982 was my statement of claiming ownership of my own life, like Esther's request to the king. I needed to ask for Peter's help to make my decision possible. Although I was careful to pay for my traveling out of my income, I needed his cooperation and commitment to our relationship in order to live with the tension caused by my travel back and forth.

I knew that I was seeking a way to integrate my sexuality more consciously. I knew, too, that my own rejection of being female would not be resolved by relating to a man. Therefore, I chose an unusual therapy experience with some other women. In the summer of 1981, while I was back in the States, I went on a "women's wilderness intensive." Twenty women camped and cooked and did process therapy together on an island in northern Minnesota. We were doing our own inner work and experiencing ways to help other women victimized by our society.

During that "wilderness intensive" not only did parental issues surface that I needed to resolve, but also the experience itself became a "vision quest" in the Native American sense. We were working with the natural environment, eating a non-addictive diet, swimming and using a sweat lodge, as well as doing therapy together.   Our therapy involved simply attending to the body process of whoever was working—from tears to sounds and body movement, waiting while images became clear, and, finally, listening while the person named what she had come to know "from the inside out."

After I had worked through a particularly heavy session and was feeling a sense of utter relaxation as a result, the massage therapist indicated that "my turn" was next. As the massage progressed, images began to fill my consciousness. First, there was the night sky, full of stars.   Then I felt myself standing on a cliff with my arms raised and my voice calling down the stars, which began to move and pour through my whole body into the earth in a never-ending stream. In my mind's eye, as dawn began to silver the sky, a name came clear: "Bird Woman." Then a great stillness was everywhere.

The next morning I did a simple thing to mark that naming. I swam all the way around our little island. No one during our visit had done that.   Later, before I had told the circle of women the story of what had happened, a friend gave me a hawk feather that she had found.   The feather seemed to confirm the name I had received.   Then I remembered that "Bird Woman" was the translation of Sacajawea, the woman I had dreamed about as a teenager.

That wilderness experience was a way to stay focused on the issue of changing structures, even though the changes were still primarily internal. Choosing to be with women in such an intimate setting de-mystified some of the issues that were plaguing me as the streams of my own life merged. I felt that I had been able to separate from my mother at a deep visceral level and to receive my own woman's name.

Your story of choosing to act beyond your own personal circle of power will be different from mine, but your naming of yourself before others is an experience we can celebrate together.   Naming yourself at each step is essential for holding onto a vision of reality that is different from the cultural interpretation of being female.

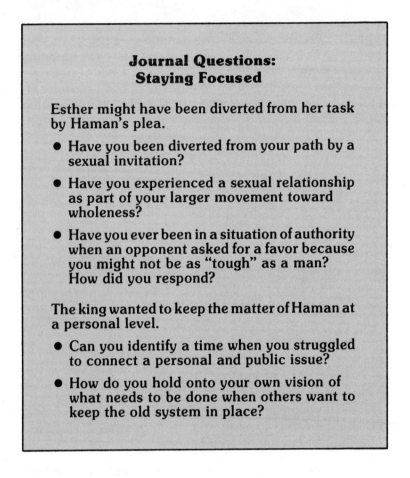

**Journal Questions:
Staying Focused**

Esther might have been diverted from her task by Haman's plea.

- Have you been diverted from your path by a sexual invitation?

- Have you experienced a sexual relationship as part of your larger movement toward wholeness?

- Have you ever been in a situation of authority when an opponent asked for a favor because you might not be as "tough" as a man? How did you respond?

The king wanted to keep the matter of Haman at a personal level.

- Can you identify a time when you struggled to connect a personal and public issue?

- How do you hold onto your own vision of what needs to be done when others want to keep the old system in place?

Identifying Community

After waiting so long to merge the braided streams of her life together—spiritual reality, gender identity and public or work role—Esther moved quickly into the mainstream of political life as an advocate for her people.

Several months after Haman's death, Esther went once again to the king's chamber to deal with the edict against her people. She knew that the king did not want to tackle the problem of undoing his own edict, but she was not going to allow him to choose a more limited favor for herself and her family.

In the process of accomplishing the larger task of saving her people, Esther began to change the way in which the laws functioned. She recognized the limits of the rigid hierarchical system that governed Persian culture, and she proposed a solution that would shift the internal power balance. Instead of urging the king to break the restrictions of his own legal system, Esther suggested that the Jews be allowed to defend themselves on the day authorized for their slaughter.

Esther made her proposal to the king out of her faith that God would not allow the Jews to be eliminated entirely. Her suggestion of struggle and defense was a participatory, dialogical and essentially creative answer to the king's static and mechanical system. What Esther proposed resembled stimulating the immune system of a living body: the embattled Jews would be allowed to fight as hard as they could within certain clear time constraints.

We are not used to choosing chaos as Esther did. It is untidy and unpredictible. Esther did not try to control the results or even the process. She asked for a kind of contained chaos! She was extending her own internal experience of opening to the possibility of death to the external realm. She could make her proposal "on faith," remembering God's faithfulness in the history of her people and the promise that they would not be obliterated. Esther knew she was called only to be faithful in doing her piece of a larger design that God was creating.

Looking at our lives with God's perspective (however we understand that statement), we can let go of having to be "in control" and, at the same time, take responsibility for doing our particular part on behalf of a larger vision. The ability to act, as Esther did, without needing to be in control depends upon doing the inner work of facing the threat of spiritual or physical death and coming to know God.

My own call to advocacy began with a question: Who are "my people?" If I want to change the institutional structures that bind or destroy them, where or to whom do I bring my request?

I know that my people are women whose gifts are not welcome in the church. I dream of the day when women and men can join hands through Christ to embody the new creation begun by Jesus. To make that dream a reality means honoring the gifts of women and changing many of the structures in the church.

My own little church, the Seekers Community at Church of the Saviour, is committed to the process of helping women and men discover their gifts for ministry. We assume that each person has a gift for the whole body (I Cor. 12:7) and that the worshipping community has the responsibility to help clarify the call of each member. Further, we are committed to the different gifts that flow out of male-female partnership and have co-pastors, Sonya Dyer and Fred Taylor, called by the congregation. The Seekers Community provides me with a corporate model for the body of Christ. My own call is to be a bridge from that congregation to others through the Women's Ministry of Faith at Work.

The Women's Ministry has provided a place for me to exercise gifts of writing and speaking, of organizing and cooperating with local teams of women who want to sponsor a Women's Event. I can name this ministry as a place to continue discovering my own gifts and an institutional base from which to address churches on behalf of new models for including women in ministry.

Extending power through non-traditional structures is one way to open up a closed system. Using access to power as Esther did, to invite a situation of controlled chaos, is another way to dissolve boundaries.

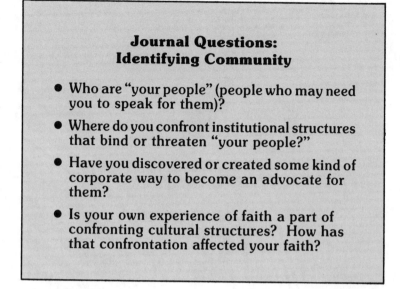

Journal Questions:
Identifying Community

- Who are "your people" (people who may need you to speak for them)?

- Where do you confront institutional structures that bind or threaten "your people?"

- Have you discovered or created some kind of corporate way to become an advocate for them?

- Is your own experience of faith a part of confronting cultural structures? How has that confrontation affected your faith?

Conclusion

Claiming one's own life as a part of claiming the right to life for others begins the process of public ministry. Esther named herself and the value of her life before the king in a very different way from Vashti. Esther stayed focused on the larger issues at hand when Haman tried to divert her with his plea for mercy. The king was ready to stay with Haman's action and move the level of Esther's request back to their personal relationship. But, Esther continued to extend her power into and through the political structure by linking the money system with the future of her people.

When the king authorized a day of defensive war all over the empire, Esther trusted God for the outcome instead of trying to control it herself. She proposed an organic remedy for a problem that had no solution within the closed legal system which the king headed. Esther stayed focused on her particular task, trusting that God would continue to reveal guidance as she lived through the events catalyzed by her actions. With each visit to the king, another break-through occurred in both private and public realms.

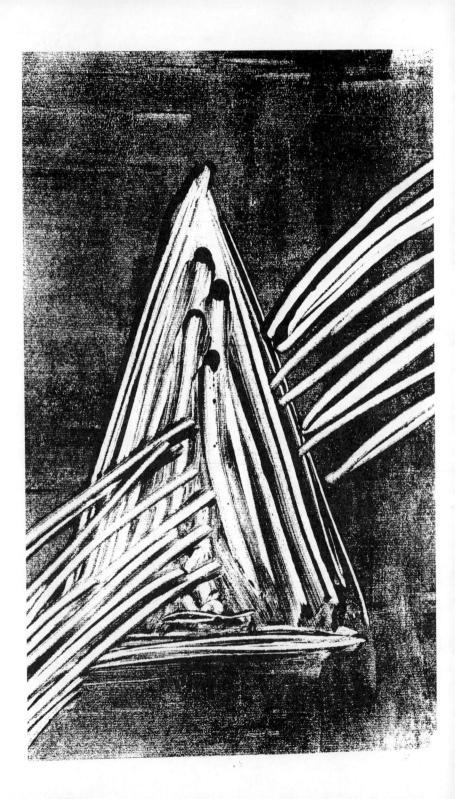

10. PARADOX OF POWER

Esther and Public Violence

Choosing a limited war to provide a realignment of power within the realm was the paradox of political power for Esther. Choosing violence stood in direct contrast to the subordinate role for women in Persian culture. War on behalf of survival always seems to be contradictory. Sometimes, when the oppressive system is too rigid to change another way, violence is necessary.

Esther's story began with the king's celebration of his many victories and Vashti's impetuous refusal to appear before the drinking warriors. At the opposite end of the story stands Esther's request for a day of war. Vashti was banished because she said "No!" to the king, and his advisors were afraid her refusal would upset the balance of male power throughout the kingdom. Esther was honored because she said "Yes!" to the full range of her power as a woman in partnership with the king, and it *did* upset the balance of power among men of the kingdom.

Choosing Violence

Esther requested a day of defensive warfare against all enemies of the Jews to counteract the unbreakable edict which Haman had persuaded the king to sign. Allowing the Jews to defend themselves would test the loyalty of the king's army, for the warriors would be present to enforce the one-day rule, not to take sides. The same men who had been present when Vashti refused to enter their banquet hall were now being ordered to carry out Esther's suggested strategy.

Because the Persian empire was so vast, the code of law was important and war was not welcomed. Control of the complex system of government filtered down from the king to every man as lord of his household. When Vashti refused to come, the king's advisors had suggested banishment, for fear that one woman in rebellion against male authority could upset the entire power structure. But, this time nobody counselled against Esther's strategy, because her influence with the king was so secure.

By the time Esther entered the political realm normally reserved for the king's advisors, Mordecai had become their chief. Esther and Mordecai moved as a team through the maze of traditions and laws that governed the empire. Their partnership secured Esther's spiritual stream in the political structures of the kingdom.

Left over from the day's of Haman's rule as the king's chief advisor, there still existed an intricate maze of loyal "henchmen" who would not support Mordecai. A one-day war would cause a violent and chaotic internal power shift in every city as local Jews replaced these officials who were loyal to Haman.

The Jews were given enough warning to prepare for the one-day war on all their enemies, and word inviting the war went out all over the kingdom. Many people converted to Judaism because it was clear that the Jews were now favored by the king. When the day came, a bloodbath ensued!

Most women reject war as a means of pursuing justice. We recognize that war is a means of enforcing uniformity instead of diversity. We know that war not only takes lives, but it also deadens human spirit.

But, we also know that articulate spirituality and personal courage in the face of violence can change human consciousness in a radical way. We remember men like Gandhi and Martin Luther King, Jr., because they made such a radical witness with their lives in the face of collective violence. We recognize that the Christ-spirit was bringing us to a new level of consciousness through them.

We remember women like Rosa Parks—the woman in Selma, Alabama, who sparked the Civil Rights movement by her symbolic refusal to give up her seat on a city bus. Rosa Parks astonished many whites who thought racial segregation was ordained by God and many blacks who thought that it would never change. Rosa Parks didn't have to do it all by herself; she acted with her body and other people responded until another area of human bondage gave way.

There is another parallel between Esther's request and the resulting violence and the vehement force of the Civil Rights Movement. Esther asked for the right of her people to defend themselves against enemies who were authorized to attack them. In our own country violence against blacks had long been tolerated or encouraged as a method of intimidation. When blacks demanded the right to defend themselves, we watched the violence erupt. Many of us were horrified by the ugly scenes on television, astounded that so much hate lay behind the laws and customs that kept us apart. When we confront a system based on violence, then violence will be part of a change as the old order struggles to maintain control.

As women, we know and often fear the violence that erupts when change takes place. We are trained to avoid conflict and so become partners in our own encasement. Men are bigger and stronger than women. Further, men often act as though they hate or worship women rather than relating to them as partners or peers. Physical differences are institutionalized to threaten women and maintain control.

Then, when we act like dolls or children or mothers, we encourage male dominance by playing out a subservient role. In the end we must enter rigid systems based on violence with enough spiritual centeredness to accept the possibility of death.

With fear and trembling, members of Church of the Saviour gather each week to march through the Adams-Morgan district of Washington, D.C. to publicize a war against drugs that is threatening to destroy the fabric of that neighborhood. It is our community protest against the vulture tactics of the drug users and dealers, against their pressure tactics which victimize individuals and isolate people from communal action.

Violence against church workers in that neighborhood simply reflects the street violence which plagues all of the residents there. We are neither more nor less protected, except that we have a way to walk together!

That single difference of walking together makes *all* the difference. The little praying communities of Church of the Saviour are spreading the corporate body of Christ in that neighborhood. We started with operating a coffee-house in the sixties and grew to restoring a housing complex for the poor in the seventies. Now that housing complex, called Jubilee Housing, has given birth to many different small pockets of community: Columbia Road Health Services, For Love of Children (FLOC), Five Loaves Bakery, Sarah's Circle housing for the elderly, and Christ's House for indigent men. Each of these places represents the servant ministry of a disciplined group of pilgrims who are committed to a combination of personal and public spiritual growth.

Members of the Church of the Saviour do confront governmental structures on behalf of a larger vision for peace. Violence does touch our community when repressive structures break. Confronting the possibility of violence together through Christ has been a source of growth for me. As long as I thought that such a witness had to be done alone, my courage failed. Now that I know we will seek God's guidance together, I can be faithful to my part and risk the violence that may come.

As long as we automatically avoid situations of potential violence, we will continue to cooperate in our own bondage. When we discover Christ in the midst of every crucifixion, we can face the possibility of death on behalf of life.

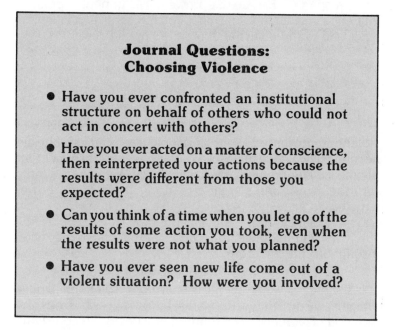

**Journal Questions:
Choosing Violence**

- Have you ever confronted an institutional structure on behalf of others who could not act in concert with others?

- Have you ever acted on a matter of conscience, then reinterpreted your actions because the results were different from those you expected?

- Can you think of a time when you let go of the results of some action you took, even when the results were not what you planned?

- Have you ever seen new life come out of a violent situation? How were you involved?

Community and Crisis

After the Jews had defended themselves all over the empire, killing their enemies and taking no plunder, Esther went in to the king yet another time. "Now what is your petition?" he asked, as though resigned to completing the change she had set in motion. "It shall be granted you" (Es. 9:12, *RSV*).

She asked that the Jews in Susa be granted one more day of killing to solidify their safety in the capital and that the ten sons of Haman be hung for all to see. This gruesome detail was symbolic of the finality of the demise of Haman's power and prosperity. His sexual prowess was gone, his political influence was ended, and his personal control over others gave way to the diversity demanded by the Jews.

The king no longer hesitated to grant Esther what she requested. His ready agreement suggested a certain resignation about his own control and a willingness to cooperate with Esther's guiding power. For Esther this second day of violence represented her political power at its fullest. She did not choose violence in order to assure her control over other people, as Haman had. Her action grew out of her identity with the Jews. She sought a rearrangement of the power structure to allow her people a viable place in it. She could choose violence because it was the only way to assure the survival of her people in the many different places they lived throughout the kingdom.

Is it violence we fear? Or is it also our isolation? Do we imagine we will have to act all by ourselves? Does the isolation of women in our modern private homes contribute to a guilty lack of confidence? What if there were others to help? What if the legal system were there to support our vision? Would we dare to imagine a better way to live—a way that would provide adequate safety, shelter and meaningful work for every person?

Perhaps in this ancient story of Esther we can find some new images for modern life. There is something debilitating about the sexual mythology in our own culture that a woman must deaden her vision and creativity to keep a husband "at home," as though coupling were the full meaning in a woman's life. We have gotten partnership confused with ownership, and we live in a cultural setting that has all but destroyed the covenant community that sustained Esther and informed the early Christians as well.

For those in my own church who are not ready to stand against repressive structures, there is a way that women of different ages and stages of development can be supportive of those who have begun to claim their advocacy roles. In the mission group structure, people are called to different tasks on behalf of the group, as well as tasks for the servant ministry each mission group has. Some people are called to tend the inner life of prayer and reflection, to stay in touch with God's presence and guidance for our work, while other members of the mission group take a more public role.

The mission group provides a place where women and men can struggle with disowned tributaries in their own lives. I have been guided and encouraged in my own spiritual journey by Sonya Dyer, one of the two pastors of the Seekers Community. Her ministry grew out of her own experience as a wife and mother. She gave leadership to *Hope and a Home,* a mission group supporting single mothers who wanted to keep their children together when poverty or legal problems threatened to destroy their families. Sonya has also worked as an equal partner with Fred Taylor in pastoring Seekers for nearly ten years.

Sonya provides me with a living model for advocacy on behalf of women in many areas. She speaks to the larger church as a lay-woman in charge of a committed and active congregation. She speaks to the city government on issues of justice for women and children. She does not avoid conflict when it comes, but she seeks to embrace diversity and to welcome the creativity of a truly corporate body of Christ. Most of all, she lives her own spiritual journey out in the open, where I can see and experience her way of living out her faith.

Do you know women like Sonya? Would it make a difference to you if you did?

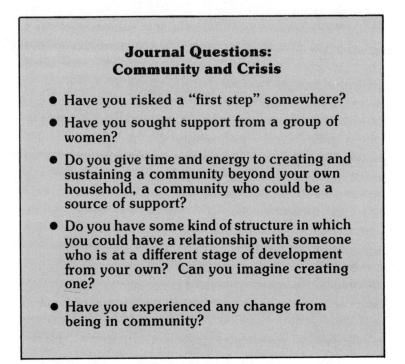

**Journal Questions:
Community and Crisis**

- Have you risked a "first step" somewhere?

- Have you sought support from a group of women?

- Do you give time and energy to creating and sustaining a community beyond your own household, a community who could be a source of support?

- Do you have some kind of structure in which you could have a relationship with someone who is at a different stage of development from your own? Can you imagine creating one?

- Have you experienced any change from being in community?

Celebration of Life

After the second day of war ended, Mordecai recorded all the events and sent a letter throughout the kingdom enjoining the Jews to keep a yearly feast of remembrance. Thus, the Feast of Purim was instituted among the Jews, and the story of Esther became a part of Hebrew mythology. From the time of Moses, tales of God's protection and deliverance sustained Jews everywhere. Now the story of God working through Esther was added to the yearly calendar of ritual celebration.

Modern Jews still celebrate Purim with gifts and good food in a party atmosphere that contrasts sharply with other seasons of ritual penitence. Purim has a feminine quality of joyful celebration and the promise of new life. It is a feast with the feeling of a birth-day!

As women, we can bring a vision for new birth to the serious work of public life. Instead of keeping our feelings and our creativity confined to the private world of home and family, as women who have experienced the convergence of streams as Esther did, we can bring the convergence of our strengths into the conscious realm of our culture. In schools and churches, hospitals and mortgage banks, women are beginning to change the male way in which "things have always been done." The creativity that women explore at home can bring new life to the tired and tiring patterns of institutional life.

Suppose we do the tough inner work that Esther did, confronting the shadowy Haman that threatens each one of us with stagnation and death. Suppose we take the steps that Esther did, beginning with an invitation to break bread with our enemies *after* a deep time of opening to God with the prayerful support of a spiritual community. Imagine how those inner changes could affect whatever work, paid or not, that we are now doing in the public sector.

Recently, a friend of mine said, "Play is when you do something and don't keep a score." Is it possible that women in our culture know how to *play*? Can you imagine bringing playfulness into our public life? Would the addition of women like Esther change the entire structure of our society?

Through Church of the Saviour and the Women's Ministry of Faith at Work, I know women who call me to play, in the sense of living without keeping an account sheet of wins and losses. Underneath the childlike word of "play," I hear the creativity of God breaking into human history. When I don't keep score, I am more likely to try something new. And, in a world where the old answers aren't providing even minimum safety or food or shelter, we desperately need to try new ways of shaping our public life together.

As I write, a group in my church community is choosing a communal answer to a newly critical problem: how to live into aging and death. They are choosing to pool their physical and mental resources, knowing there is real hardship and real joy that will come out of their differences. They will live together in the same building, sharing worship, food, learning activities and nursing care. They are giving birth to a new form of family right in the middle of Washington, D.C.

All around me I am seeing a new level of consciousness about unique qualities that women bring to every organizational structure I know. Hope is everywhere in the small clusters of women who are entering public life. And, at the same time, I am seeing Haman's shadow everywhere, clouding the horizon with threat and war.

In the clusters that have a spiritual center, I see a new awareness of the need for celebration in the midst of trials and set-backs. Just as the Jews need to celebrate Purim each year to recall the way in which God acts, we need a time of giving thanks for life itself to continue to open us to new possibilities and new hope.

Journal Questions: Celebration of Life

- Have you ever said "Yes" to an institutional task that seemed too difficult for you?

- Has there been a way to celebrate your risk-taking, no matter what the outcome was!

- Are you conscious of the importance of ritual in your life? In your community?

Conclusion

The paradox of violence as a part of changing a rigid cultural system is not one that can be resolved. Instead, conflicting values must be held in tension as our understanding of God at work through human beings enlarges. We seek peaceful ways of changing structures to bring justice and equality to all women, and, yet, we recognize that violence may result when a rigid system cracks. Celebration of the Eucharist reminds us that Jesus faced the same paradox. If we believe that God indeed lives among us enlarging our vision of justice for all, then we will continue to celebrate life in the midst of death.

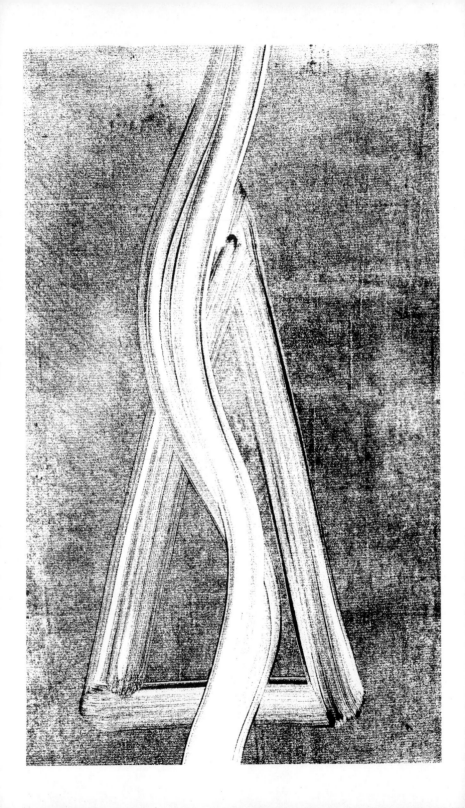

11. LIKE A RIVER FLOWING...

Four braided streams run together as a flowing river from the past into the future: Esther's stream, our collective stream as women, my personal stream, and your individual stream. Esther's stream began with the culture to which she was born, and it ended with the war that cracked a closed political system wide open. Our history as American women is just beginning to be written, as women enter public life with a different vision and a different way of operating "from the inside out." My own divided streams have come together, running faster in my part of God's unfolding creation. Your story is the silent stream, but it is still a part of the river of joined streams.

Esther's Story

From the headwaters of the Persian culture to which she was born, Esther learned the cultural expectations for herself as a female. As a very beautiful woman, she learned her power to please the king. As a Jew and adopted daughter of Mordecai, she learned to be obedient; she listened when he told her to deny her Jewish heritage. Esther learned to cooperate with the dominant male version of being a woman, and she learned to deny what did not fit that picture. The stream of her personhood began to split into three separate, braided streams: being female, being Jewish, and being the queen.

Esther must have heard the story of Vashti, the queen whom she replaced, told as a warning against refusing the king. Underneath, the rebellion of Vashti carried a message for Esther—the idea that is was possible (though dangerous) to say "No!" to the cultural image of being an object, a plaything, a slave to the king. The story of Vashti carried seeds of nascent selfhood.

The spiritual heritage of Mordecai gave Esther a different context for her actions from the cultural conventions. Out of the history and traditions of a covenant relationship with God, as well as out of the sense of Mordecai's living relationship with God through dreams and ritual prayer, Esther stood with one foot in her culture and one foot in God's eternal now, although she did not recognize her split position fully until the crisis of Haman's edict came.

Hagai helped Esther to connect her sexual role with her own body by schooling her in the sensuality that women were supposed to bring to the king's bed. Hegai's advice to Esther when she went in to the king's chamber was a powerful affirmation of her self, grounded in her body: he encouraged her to go in "unadorned."

At the convergence of Esther's three braided streams stood Mordecai in sackcloth and ashes, confronting Esther with the choice that she had to make. "Who knows," Mordecai wrote to her, "whether you have not come to the kingdom for such a time as this?" (Es. 4:14, *RSV*). With those words Mordecai was challenging her to move beyond her cultural limits as the queen, to risk her own covenant relationship with God on behalf of the Jewish people, and to own her full power as a woman.

After initially denying that she would have to make such a choice, Esther moved from her partial identity as a wife to her full identity as a woman. From the tributary streams of her female body, her Hebrew faith, and her role in the Persian court, Esther withdrew into a time of fasting and prayer that was symbolic of disappearing from the external roles that had defined her previously. She figuratively descended into the bowels of the earth and cried out to God: "Free me from my fear, for I am about to take my life in my hands!" (Es. 4:17l, *JB*).

Then, as though starting up a mirror-image pathway, Esther began by presenting her body for the king's mercy. As if she was following the opposite of Hegai's advice to enter the king's bedroom "unadorned," Esther dressed herself in all her robes and approached the throne with a new-found confidence within herself.

When the king granted her the favor of being received instead of having her killed, Esther moved to the mirror-image of Mordecai's spiritual heritage by inviting her enemies to her own table. Symbolically, Esther surrounded Haman and the king with her own reality: the food she served, the place she lived and the God she knew so intimately. Haman and the king continued to operate from their own more limited sense of reality and control, but Esther's intimate relationship with God meant that she could use her spiritual sensitivity to wait for God's timing.

As Esther extended her sense of balance and timing into the actual request for the life of her people, she was acting as a counterpart to Vashti's lonely rebellion. As Esther became more sure of herself, she identified with "her people" and continued to press the king on their behalf, even when he wanted to limit his favor to Esther and her family. Her positive action was just the obverse of Vashti's pattern. Like a child, Vashti refused to come when she was called. Like a full-grown woman, Esther chose to walk where she was forbidden to go.

In the end of the story, Mordecai remembered his dream of the two dragons and the cry that became a mighty river. "Esther was the river," he wrote, "The dragons are Haman and myself" (Es. 10:3, *JB*). What a strong image! Esther was a river that began with a cry, like a fissure in the earth with tears spilling out. Her own power as a woman began with just the cry of anguish and fear and faith! Esther was a river in the king's land, bringing God's power through her own being. She did not seek to destroy the king's power, but her own life changed his closed and rigid political system. She did not ask for half of the kingdom; instead, she claimed the inner realm of her soul. She did not eschew political power, but her public role was only part of the richness she discovered as the river began to flow faster and fuller.

A Woman's Way of Growing

The image of male dominance, clearly implied by Esther's story, is that men left alone and in charge of public life become dragons, like Haman and Mordecai. If the church is to be a living embodiment of God, then we must find ways to create new and more flexible structures that will embrace our sexual dynamics and differences. We must allow the cry of oppressed people to swell and grow in our midst, not to destroy the dragons but to fill out the picture of how God works.

A woman's way of growing is different from a man's. Esther's braided stream was like that of most women. The combination of cultural context and dissociation of sexuality from body-knowing makes women vulnerable to living in separated streams. We need to make a conscious effort to create the structures through which women can enter public life as powerful integrated women like Esther finally became.

Mordecai's dream of Esther as a river between two dragons is a powerful and creative image. Always in motion, a river dissolves, erodes, changes the face of dry land. In mythology a river marks the border between one state of consciousness and another.

In her book *Diving Deep and Surfacing,* Carol Christ writes that a woman's spiritual quest begins with an experience of *nothingness.* At the point of nothingness in Esther's journey, she had left behind all of the men who had told her who she was and why she was alive. For three days, as though in a tomb of stone or at the bottom of the ocean, Esther sought the courage to choose life fully.

Esther opened herself to partnering with God when she recalled the story of God's guidance and mercy in earlier times and confessed the sin of her people in forgetting that promise. She stood before God as a priest and a prophet, a connecting link in her own person. Without preconceptions, she allowed God to work as a creative artist through her simple, even foolish, act of asking the king to dinner.

The question of how God works in the world is focused by Esther's prayer. There is something in her own remembering that is necessary for activating God's revelation. Without Esther, can God remember? Is the ability to reflect on our experiences an essential quality of being made in the likeness of God? And is our ability to perceive God enhanced by female *and* male knowing?

Discerning the true nature of God is part of Esther's story. In contrast to the closed system which the king controlled, God worked through Esther and through dreams to bring about change. My waking dream for the church is that we will find ways to welcome the "riverness" of women. God seems willing to honor the creativity and converging streams of women, but our cultural institutions (including the church) often seem fearful of embracing change, and many remain closed to full partnership with women. Many times the church has been part of the cultural structure for limiting development of women.

By dissociating body and spirit, the church has neglected soul development that includes all the tributary streams that Esther lived. If we take our Biblical heritage seriously, then we can learn a more wholistic image of God from the story of Esther, as well as understand more about the tributary streams of a woman's spiritual development.

My Life Like a River

Having come from the Pacific Northwest, the rivers in my life are swift and cold. They are loud and full of energy to drive electric power plants. They nourish the volcanic soil in eastern Washington to produce miles of wheat and provide spawning ground for the salmon that come back from the ocean to breed. They destroy and erode in flood-times; they feed and create in due season. My rivers are alive with particular character and universal energy.

During most of my adult life, I lived in three different, braided streams: the streams of work, spirit, and being female. These streams always ran on the rocky ground of male values and my father's judgment. During the tumultuous year after I turned forty, my three braided streams merged and ran together as I faced surgery alone. Since then, I have moved outward from my body as a spiritual center, one stage at a time—from personal power, to advocacy for others through the Women's Ministry of Faith at Work, to confronting the oppressive structures of our society through the mission group communities of Church of the Saviour.

On the morning I finished writing this book, I woke up with a dream of a picture-perfect mountain, its snowy cap glowing reddish-pink in dawn or sunset, rising out of a dark bay. As I stared at the mountain, wondering whether it was morning or evening, a first-grade boy tugged at my hand.

"Mommy, if dad goes to court, will they send me with him and let you keep Tina?"

"Do you want to stay with me, Tommy?" He nodded. "Both of you can stay with me." He smiled, satisfied, and we both stared at the mountain. Then I awoke.

The mountain in my dream was shaped like Mt. Ranier, rising out of Puget Sound. I grew up in the land between the Cascade Mountains, where Mt. Ranier is located, and the Pacific waters of Puget Sound. My father was like that mountain, a triangular form as solid as stone. My mother was like the dark water, always changing. I lived my life between them, physically and emotionally.

In the dream I was standing on an island, looking back at the mainland. I was no longer between the mountain and the bay. I remembered the women's wilderness intensive, the experience of receiving my own name, and swimming around the island to mark the event. The dream brought that naming into the present: Bird Woman, as explorer.

For me this dream is a symbol of completion, because I am at a different place in the scene from the place in which I grew up. I believe the dream marks the completion of an important phase in my spiritual journey.

The little boy tugging at my wrist seemed anxious that, at this point in my life, I would prefer the smaller girl child. I know that little boy well. He is my inner child. The little girl is younger, newer, and the boy is right to feel anxious because I love her more right now. She is new to my soul, cherished and held close.

When I awoke from that dream, I knew that it was full of integration images. My inner parental images were there in nature, and my inner masculine and feminine sides were there as children. Although I could not decide in the dream whether it was morning or evening, my ego self was clear about welcoming both children to stay with me now. Doing the task of writing this book has been an important ending and beginning for me. I feel as if I have been away for a long time and now I have come home to my body. Coming home to my body is coming home to God.

Journal Questions:
Your Life Like a River

- Draw the river of your own life, with its tributary streams, major currents, rocks and dams.

- Add any features you want to explore: perhaps a barrier coming up or nearby features about to break through into your river.

- Let your imagination explore the fullness of this image.

Conclusion

We have taken a journey with Esther, through the inter-woven, braided streams of her life and ours. I hope you will share the journal questions with other women in your own community. As women we need to write our own stories and tell them aloud and dance them together and sing them out to the world. If we believe that we are the growing edge of God, our understanding has enormous implications for how we live with each other and the rest of creation. As women we embody an important part of God's image! Let us begin to live as the river flowing between dragons, full of the power to change and create new patterns of life on this earth.

BIBLIOGRAPHY

Books have been my companions for a spiritual journey that has been rather solitary. As I moved from place to place with my husband Peter, there were not always people with whom I could talk, so I read and kept a journal. Particular books that prepared the way for writing *Braided Streams* are listed in this section, with comments about how these authors informed my own thinking. This book list is not exhaustive or particularly systematic, but it may be helpful for your own reading and reflecting.

Boulding, Elise. **The Underside of History.** Boulder: Westview, 1976.

> *An overview of women in history, constructed from fragments to supplement standard chronologies and court records which largely ignored the role of women.*

Briggs, Dorothy Corkille. **Celebrate Yourself.** Garden City, NY: Doubleday and Co., 1977.

> *A basic book for learning to affirm one's own life. I found chapter 12, "Making Coupleship Work," especially useful during my own convergence period. The checklist of basic ideas provides a summary and guideline for women making the perilous transition from wife to woman.*

Brueggemann, Walter. **The Prophetic Imagination.** Philadelphia: Fortress Press, 1978.

> *Brueggemann's discussion of Moses stimulated my thinking about the Jews as an alternative community to the "royal consciousness" that dominates culture.*

Christ, Carol P. **Diving Deep and Surfacing: Women Writers on Spiritual Quest.** Boston: Beacon Press, 1980.

> *A discussion of five women writers, this book defines elements of a woman's spiritual quest as: the experience of nothingness, mystical awakenings (in nature), new naming, emergence of sacred story and women's rituals to celebrate body, nature, feeling and intuition.*

Claremont de Castillejo, Irene. **Knowing Woman: a Feminine Psychology.** New York: Harper and Row, 1973.

> *The distinction which Castillejo makes between diffused awareness in "the feminine" and focused consciousness in "the masculine" helped me to see the wholeness in Esther's way of operating within the political arena. The chapters on "The Rainmaker Ideal" and "The Older Woman" are a celebration of aging in women who have done their inner work.*

Dinnerstein, Dorothy. **The Mermaid and the Minotaur: Sexual Arrangements and Human Malaise.** New York: Harper and Row, 1976.

> *A provocative polemic challenging men to share the work of child-rearing as the way to change attitudes about women in our culture.*

Eichenbaum, Luise and Orbach, Susie. **What Do Women Want: Exploding the Myth of Dependency.** New York: Berkley Books, 1983.

> *Describing women as care-givers from the very first, the authors make a case for teaching men those skills as well as learning to receive care from other women (chapter VI).*

Erikson, Erik. **Childhood and Society.** New York: W.W. Norton and Co., 1950.

> *After describing different play patterns for girls and boys, Erikson drops women from his standard interpretation of adult ego development called "Eight Stages of Man." This is still basic reading for the standard cultural interpretation of developmental stages.*

Gilligan, Carol. **In a Different Voice: Psychological Theory and Women's Development.** Cambridge: Harvard University Press, 1982.

> *A critique of the standard interpretation of human development by Erikson and Kohlberg, Gilligan provides an empirical observation of the patterns women exhibit in moral development, moving from relationship toward autonomy.*

The Interpreter's Bible, Vol. III. New York: Abingdon, 1954.

Jung, C.G. **Memories, Dreams, Reflections.** New York: Vintage, 1965.

> *An autobiographical reflection on Jung's long life and inward spiritual quest, this is a good introduction to the mature thought of Jung.*

Kelsey, Morton. **Transcend: a Guide to the Spiritual Quest.** New York: Crossroad, 1981.

> *Just one of this profilic writer's many books on the inward journey, chapters 2 and 3 on welcoming spiritual reality with a materialistic worldview were particularly useful as I thought about the different realities of Haman and Mordecai.*

Kolbenschlag, Madonna. **Kiss Sleeping Beauty Good-Bye: Breaking the Spell of Feminine Myths and Models.** New York: Bantam Books, 1981.

> *This book helped me understand Vashti's desperate refusal as an act of awakening. It should be on every woman's bookshelf!*

Koller, Alice. **An Unknown Woman: a Journey to Self-Discovery.** New York: Bantam Books, 1983.

> *This is her story of converging streams after long separation of sexual and vocational strands from her body and spiritual self.*

McFague, Sallie. **Metaphorical Theology: Models of God in Religious Language.** Philadelphia: Fortress Press, 1982.

> *This book gave me courage to trust my own intuition about the importance of Esther's story as a "model of God."*

Needleman, Jacob. **A Sense of the Cosmos: the Encounter of Modern Science and Ancient Truth.** New York: E. P. Dutton and Co., 1965.

> *Although this is an "old" book among current descriptions of New Age physics, Needleman connects science and religion through his critical mind, challenging me to stretch my own consciousness by attending expectantly to all of my experience.*

O'Connor, Elizabeth. **Eighth Day of Creation: Gifts and Creativity.** Waco, TX: Word Books, 1971.

> *A course on discovering gifts for ministry that has been used for many years at Church of the Saviour in Washington, D.C., the exerpts from other books provide an excellent bibliography that nourished my soul for years before I got to this church.*

Orwell, George. **Nineteen-Eighty-Four.** New York: Harcourt Brace, 1949.

> *This classic story of controlling records and rewriting history as a way to control people describes Haman's reality in contemporary society.*

Richards, M.C. **Centering in Pottery, Poetry and the Person.** Middletown, CN: Wesleyan University Press, 1962.

> *A celebration of life, this was the beginning for me.!*

Russell, Letty M. **Human Liberation in a Feminist Perspective: A Theology.** Philadelphia: Westminster Press, 1974.

> *This book is a coherent and challenging theology of wholeness in the image of God and partnership between male and female in the church.*

Sanford, John A. **Dreams: God's Forgotten Language.** New York: J.B. Lippincott Co., 1968.

> *A good discussion of the relevance of dreams to Christian experience, this book also has a description of key Biblical dreams.*

Sangiuliano, Iris. **In Her Time.** New York: Morrow Quill Paperbacks, 1980.

> *Discovering this book almost dissuaded me from writing mine, because she also used life-lines to discuss different patterns for women's lives. It's an encouraging and realistic book, based on case histories of women coming to self-consciousness.*

Scarf, Maggie. **Unfinished Business: Pressure Points in the Lives of Women.** New York: Ballantine Books, 1980.

> *Arranged by decades, this book begins as a study of depression among women and becomes a description of the unfinished developmental business at each stage of life.*

Schaef, Anne Wilson. **Women's Reality: an Emerging Female System in the White Male Society.** Minneapolis: Winston Press, 1981.

> At first this book seemed too angry and simplistic about the differences women experience in our society, but the longer I live with Anne Schaef's categories, the more I can choose my own reality within the Male System of our culture.

Stahl, Carolyn. **Opening to God: Guided Imagery Meditation on Scripture.** The Upper Room, 1977.

> An excellent introduction to the use of guided imagery for connecting Scripture with life.

Ulanov, Ann Belford. **The Feminine in Jungian Psychology and in Christian Theology.** Evanston: Northwestern University Press, 1971.

> A discussion of "the feminine" in men and women at different stages of psycho-spiritual development, I appreciated her interpretation of Jung's ideas and her analysis of "the feminine" and the Christian doctrine of the trinity.

Washbourn, Penelope. **Becoming Woman: a Quest for Wholeness in Female Experience.** New York: Harper and Row, 1977.

> This book started me thinking about body changes as the focal point for a woman's spiritual development.

Marjory Zoet Bankson

- *President of Faith at Work, Columbia, Maryland*
- *professional potter*
- *gifted teacher and retreat leader*
- *member, The Church of The Saviour, Washington D.C.*
- *wife of Peter R. Bankson*

Graduate of Radcliffe College with honors in American government, Marjory has a Masters degree in history from the University of Alaska. She taught school and was the women's counselor at Dartmouth College before she became a full-time potter in 1970.

In the decade between 1970 and 1980, Marjory maintained a professional pottery studio while she explored classical spiritual disciplines and taught in the School of Christian Living at The Church of The Saviour. Now a member of the Seekers, one of the worshipping communities in that unique church, Marjory preaches regularly and continues to teach classes in the school.

Since 1980, when the Banksons were transferred to Germany, Marjory has been writing and speaking at ecumenical gatherings:

- keynote speaker, Protestant Women of the Chapel Conference for all of Europe, at Bechtesgarden, West Germany
- keynoter, Disciples of Christ, Rocky Mountain Region
- main speaker, Presbyterian Synodical of Lakes and Prairies
- main speaker, Diocese of Southern Virginia Christian Education Conference at Shrinemont
- speaker, East Coast Clinical Pastoral Education Supervisor's Retreat

Involved in the inception of the Women's Ministry of Faith at Work, Marjory has designed and shared leadership of many FAW Women's Events. In January, 1986, she was selected to be the President of Faith at Work, a nationwide ministry of experiential faith and renewal for the church.

Married since 1961, Marjory brings a richness of life experience, skill at teaching, and a potter's hand to her ministry.

BRAIDED STREAMS: LEADER'S GUIDE

by Lura Jane Geiger
with Pat Backman

A complete guide for women's study groups, based on the popular **Braided Streams** by Marjory Zoet Bankson. In clear, outlined format, this 10-session course (2½ hours per session) utilizes Bible study, centering, guided imagery, creative coloring experiences and group growth exercises. Groups that have already been using **Braided Streams** for study will find that this course outline offers new resources to enrich the growth journey. It is a course that is exciting, enabling, healing and gentle; a way to help women braid the streams of their lives within a women's support group.

The **Braided Streams Leader's Guide** includes complete explanations of methods and processes, preparatory work for each session (which can be duplicated for group members), and an extensive bibliography.

CONTENTS

Settling In: to get acquainted and make a group covenant
Reference Points: to look at ways your life differs from cultural norms
Identity — Self: to appreciate the importance of your name
Identity — Community: to reflect upon people who evoked your gifts
Identity — Sexual: to examine and integrate the male and female within
Security vs. Risk: to consider the supports needed for risking new life
Integration: to make room for God
Resistance & Release: to explore different kinds of power
Confrontation & Healing: to value confrontation in love as a healing process
New Life: to celebrate your new life in community

8½" x 11". Spiral-bound Text. ISBN 0-931055-09-1

Lura Jane Geiger - Therapist, writer, teacher; leader of groups, classes and retreats; publisher of LuraMedia books for personal growth.

Pat Backman - Chaplain, Episcopal Community Services, San Diego, California; Biblical scholar, teacher and retreat leader.